dine in

dine in

Adam Newell

NH

NEW
HOLLAND

foreword

During my long career, a great many young, aspiring chefs have come through our kitchens. I cannot say I remember them all. Adam – who I remember so well – is one of the few who I knew from the very beginning was going to have a brilliant career.

Adam's latest book, *Dine In*, is a source of inspiration for people who might have previously been afraid (and there are quite a few of them) to cook for a group of people. The simplicity of the recipes speak for themselves. They will also allow you, when you have a party at home, to spend time with your guests rather than be chained to the stove.

Well done, Adam. The team at Le Gavroche remembers you with fondness.

Albert H Roux OBE

introduction

I love having friends and family around for a meal and creating an atmosphere that makes everyone smile. I get such a buzz out of seeing people digging in and enjoying themselves. It doesn't matter whether it's a simple meal or something more complicated; people will always appreciate it when you cook with passion.

When I think back to what my mother and grandmother used to cook, I realise their choices were probably easier because of the smaller range of ingredients available to them compared to what we can buy today. And the current return to cooking with local food seems to me to indicate that a lot of people would prefer to return to this much simpler way of shopping and eating.

Dine In is arranged according to the kind of meals you might want to serve when entertaining at home; from brunch to a late supper. There are complicated recipes to impress and some simple ones too, such as cheese on toast, which is fantastic if made with well-flavoured cheese, ripe tomatoes and fresh herbs.

When you're planning an event or meal, think it through carefully and keep it simple enough to handle without undue stress. But don't be put off trying something new. Once you've mastered a few dishes, there's nothing wrong with cooking them again and again; I would rather go round for one of my mother-in-law's roast chickens and the world's crispiest roast potatoes than have her attempt something she'd seen on *Iron Chef America*!

Entertaining people doesn't have to be an elaborate business unless you want it to be. The important thing is to enjoy sharing time with family and friends.

brunch

Brunch-type dishes are some of my favourites. Nothing has to be too serious – it's more about having family and friends over to chat and unwind. Keeping the food simple and relying on good ingredients will take the stress out of the occasion, giving you time to relax.

Grilled Haloumi, Poached Eggs & Basil on English Muffins

Serves 6

Perfect for summertime when tomatoes and basil are at their best, this dish is very easy to make for a quick brunch meal.

6 English muffins
1 red chilli, finely diced
24 thin slices haloumi cheese
6 ripe vine tomatoes, finely sliced
1 red onion, finely sliced
salt and pepper
1 cup basil leaves
12 free-range eggs
70ml extra virgin olive oil and
  2 tbsp chopped chives to serve

Preheat the oven to 180°C.

Split the muffins in half and rub the cut sides with the diced chilli.

Place a slice of haloumi on each muffin half, cover with tomato and red onion slices and season. Scatter several basil leaves on top, followed by another slice of haloumi.

Place the muffins on a tray and bake until golden and the cheese has nicely melted, about 3–4 minutes. While the muffins are baking, lightly poach the eggs in batches of four or six until soft and drain on kitchen paper.

TO SERVE

Place two muffin halves in the centre of each plate and top each with a poached egg. Drizzle with the oil, scatter the chopped chives on top and finish with a grind of black pepper.

Classic Kedgeree

Serves 6

This easy-to-make version of the famed breakfast comfort food shouldn't be made too spicy or you'll mask the flavour of the smoked fish. Also, don't stir the rice too much as you would for a risotto or it will become mushy.

2 onions, finely chopped

2 cloves garlic, finely chopped

150g unsalted butter

3 tsp red curry paste

2 cups basmati rice

1.2 litres chicken stock, heated

salt and pepper

720g smoked snapper (or any other flaky white fish)

50ml extra virgin olive oil

1 cup chopped flat-leaf parsley

zest and juice of 1 lemon

6 free-range eggs, hard-boiled, peeled and halved lengthways to garnish

3 lemons, cut into wedges to garnish

Sauté the onions and garlic in the butter in a heavy-bottomed saucepan, and cook without colouring until soft.

Add the curry paste and cook for 2 minutes. Add the rice and mix in well, then add the hot stock. Season to taste. Bring to a simmer, cover with a lid and cook over a very low heat, stirring occasionally, until the rice is fluffy, about 10–12 minutes.

Preheat the oven to 180°C. While the rice is cooking, flake the fish and place on a baking tray. Drizzle with the oil and bake for 5–10 minutes or until hot.

At the last minute, add the fish, parsley, lemon zest and juice to the rice.

TO SERVE

Divide between six bowls, garnish with the egg halves and lemon wedges and take to the table immediately. Serve with curry sauce on the side if desired.

Crayfish & Baked Eggs with Lemon Mayonnaise

Serves 6

With all the hard work done beforehand, this very simple brunch dish is made in individual flan dishes which enable the eggs to cook quickly. If crayfish is not available, it's also great with smoked salmon or white crabmeat.

BAKED EGGS

1 x 1kg cooked crayfish

salt and pepper

zest of 1 lemon

6 tbsp sour cream

2 cups wilted spinach, well drained and seasoned with salt and pepper

1 tbsp chopped dill

1 tbsp chopped capers

12 free-range eggs

100ml cream

LEMON MAYONNAISE

zest and juice of 2 lemons

1 tbsp castor sugar

4 egg yolks

1 tbsp Dijon mustard

2 cloves garlic

1½ cups olive oil

salt and pepper

chopped dill and grilled bread to serve

Preheat the oven to 160°C.

Remove the meat from the crayfish tail and legs and divide evenly between six individual 10–12cm flan dishes or ramekins. Season with salt and pepper and the lemon zest.

Spread 1 tablespoon of sour cream over the crayfish in each dish, then spread the spinach on top, covering the crayfish and sour cream. Sprinkle with the dill and capers.

Crack two eggs on top of the spinach in each dish and season to taste.

Bake until the eggs are half cooked. Remove from the oven and cover with cream. Return to the oven and continue baking until cooked.

To make the mayonnaise, combine the lemon zest, juice and sugar in a saucepan and bring to the boil, then allow to cool.

Blend the egg yolks, mustard, cooled lemon mixture and the garlic in a food processor on high speed for 1 minute. With the motor running, slowly drizzle in the olive oil in a thin, steady stream until well incorporated. Season with salt and pepper.

TO SERVE

Sprinkle each dish with some chopped dill and serve with the lemon mayonnaise and grilled bread.

Lamb & Onion Bhajis with Cucumber Dip

Serves 6

These little morsels are great for hangovers: nice and spicy and easy to make. Ensure the oil isn't too hot or they'll end up dark on the outside and uncooked on the inside. You can easily substitute pork for the lamb, which works just as well.

LAMB & ONION BHAJIS

100g lean lamb mince

1 medium red onion, chopped

small bunch of spinach, cooked, drained and chopped

35g chickpea flour

1 tsp finely diced fresh ginger

1 tsp coriander seeds, toasted and ground

1 tbsp chopped fresh mint

½ green chilli, deseeded and finely diced

water

1 tsp salt

pinch of red chilli powder

pinch of turmeric

sunflower oil for frying

CUCUMBER DIP

1 cucumber, peeled, deseeded and chopped finely (or grated)

2 tbsp runny honey

2 tbsp chopped fresh mint

1 tbsp white wine vinegar

½ tsp fresh red chilli, chopped

1 cup thick Greek-style yoghurt

salt and pepper

chopped fresh mint and coriander to garnish

Mix together the lamb, onion, spinach, chickpea flour, ginger, ground coriander seeds, mint and chilli along with enough water to bind into a thick batter.

Add the salt, chilli powder and turmeric and mix thoroughly.

Add enough sunflower oil to a wok so that it comes about 2.5cm up the sides, and heat.

Gently drop a little of the bhaji mixture into the hot oil to test if it's hot enough (it should sizzle).

When ready, place golf ball-sized amounts of the mixture into the oil. Reduce the heat and fry gently until golden in colour. Remove from the oil and drain on kitchen paper.

Increase the heat, return the cooked bhajis to the wok and fry in the oil for a second time until crisp and golden brown.

To make the dip, combine all the ingredients and allow to infuse in the fridge for 1–2 hours before serving.

TO SERVE

Sprinkle the bhajis with the chopped herbs and serve with the cucumber dip.

Pissaladière

Serves 6

Similar to a giant pizza cooked in a tray using puff pastry for the base, this is a classic Provençal dish and reminds me of time I've spent in Cannes. Make sure you use good quality anchovies and olives – it'll make all the difference.

100ml extra virgin olive oil

2½ white onions, thinly sliced

4 cloves garlic, chopped

2 tsp fresh thyme leaves

pinch of chilli flakes

flaky salt and cracked black pepper

500g puff pastry

12 plump anchovy fillets

50g Kalamata olives, pitted and halved

2 tbsp chopped flat-leaf parsley

freshly grated Parmesan cheese to taste

extra virgin olive oil to serve

Preheat the oven to 200°C.

In a large heavy-bottomed saucepan, heat the oil over a medium-high heat. Add the onions and garlic and slowly cook until nicely caramelised. Add the thyme and chilli flakes and cook for a further 2–3 minutes. Season with salt and pepper and remove from the heat. Allow to cool in the fridge.

Lightly grease a large baking tray. Roll out the puff pastry to line the base and about 5mm up the sides. Prick the base with a fork, then evenly cover it with the cold onion mixture. Arrange the anchovy fillets in a criss-cross pattern over the onion and place an olive in each of the diamond shapes.

Bake until the pastry is golden brown, about 20–25 minutes.

Remove from the oven and sprinkle with the chopped parsley and Parmesan. Drizzle with the oil and serve warm.

Polenta & Bacon Sandwiches with Celeriac Slaw

Serves 6

This recipe uses well-flavoured set polenta as an alternative to bread in the sandwich, which is great for people who can't eat gluten.

POLENTA

1.3 litres chicken stock
salt and pepper
200g instant polenta
50g Parmesan cheese, grated

SANDWICHES

2 tbsp Dijon mustard
24 thin slices mozzarella cheese
100g rocket
12 slices thin pancetta or
   bacon, grilled
80g Parmesan cheese, grated
2 tbsp chopped chives
butter

CELERIAC SLAW

2 celeriac, peeled and julienned
salt
2 tbsp wholegrain mustard
bunch of chives, chopped
4 tbsp mayonnaise
juice of 1 lemon
salt and pepper

extra virgin olive oil to serve

Bring the stock to the boil and season with salt and pepper. Slowly pour in the polenta, stirring continuously to avoid lumps. Cook for 3 minutes or until the polenta is thick and no longer grainy. Add the Parmesan and mix it in until it has melted.

Line a 30cm x 40cm shallow oven tray with cling film. Pour the polenta into the tray on top of the cling film and spread out evenly to a depth of about 1cm. Refrigerate until set, about 30 minutes.

When set, cut the polenta into 12 circles, using a large round pastry cutter.

Preheat the oven to 180°C. Place six slices of polenta on a greased oven tray and brush with half the Dijon mustard. Top each with two slices of mozzarella, a handful of rocket and two slices of pancetta. Sprinkle with Parmesan and chives and top with another two slices of mozzarella.

Brush the remaining polenta slices with Dijon mustard and place, mustard side down, on the cheese-topped polenta to make six sandwiches.

Place a knob of butter on top of each sandwich, then place in the oven and bake until golden brown on top. Turn the sandwiches over, lightly pressing each one after turning, and bake until this side is also golden brown.

To make the slaw, season the chopped celeriac with salt and leave for 20 minutes, then squeeze out any excess water. Add the remaining ingredients, mixing to combine well, and season with salt and pepper.

TO SERVE

Cut each sandwich in half and drizzle with the oil. Serve with a large spoonful of the celeriac slaw.

Omelette Arnold Bennett

Serves 6

A flat, Spanish-style omelette that gets its name from the novelist Arnold Bennett because this is exactly how he used to order it to be prepared at Claridge's Hotel in London.

CHEESE SAUCE

30g butter

30g plain flour

400ml hot milk

60g Cheddar cheese, grated

a little English mustard

dash of Worcestershire sauce

salt and pepper

4 tbsp whipped cream

1 egg yolk

OMELETTE

400g smoked haddock (or your favourite smoked fish)

juice of 1 lemon

8 medium free-range eggs

salt and pepper

50g butter

chopped flat-leaf parsley and lemon wedges to garnish

Start by making the cheese sauce. Melt the butter in a heavy-bottomed saucepan, add the flour and cook for 2–3 minutes, stirring slowly. Gradually whisk in the hot milk, bring to the boil and simmer for a further 2–3 minutes. Remove from the heat and add all the other ingredients except the cream and egg yolk. Stir until the cheese has melted. Cover with cling film and set aside to keep warm.

Steam the smoked fish over a double boiler until heated through. Sprinkle with lemon juice and set aside to keep warm.

Whisk the eggs and season with salt and pepper. Heat the butter in a non-stick frying pan. Pour in the eggs and place over a low heat until half-cooked – they should still be very runny in the middle.

Fold the cream and egg yolk into the warm cheese sauce. Sprinkle the omelette with the steamed fish, top with the cheese sauce then slide it onto an ovenproof plate and cook under a preheated grill for a few minutes until the top turns golden brown.

Serve with the parsley and lemon wedges.

Roast Figs with Oranges & Honey Mascarpone

Serves 6

Very easy to make, this autumn dessert relies on fantastic fresh figs and oranges. I've used mascarpone here but vanilla bean, walnut or hazelnut ice cream are all good substitutes.

12 fresh figs

60ml Grand Marnier

100ml dry white wine

3 oranges, peeled and cut into segments

500g mascarpone

2 tbsp clear honey

2 tbsp roughly chopped roasted almonds

Preheat the oven to 200°C.

Cut a cross in each fig, only cutting one-third of the way through. Place the figs in an ovenproof dish and pour in the Grand Marnier and wine. Arrange the orange segments around the figs.

Bake for 10 minutes until the figs are soft. Remove the figs and oranges from the syrup and set aside to cool to room temperature, reserving the syrup.

Lightly mix together the mascarpone and honey, then fold in the almonds.

TO SERVE

Arrange the figs and oranges on a serving dish. Drizzle over the syrup. Place a spoonful of the mascarpone mixture next to each fig and serve.

Rhubarb & Vanilla Cobbler

Serves 6

A true English classic, this cobbler is one of my mum's specialties. She also makes wonderful breads and cakes, but her scones, placed on top of stewed fruit then baked, were always a favourite in our house. It's magic as an autumnal or winter dessert, or try it in summer with apples or pears and red fruit.

STEWED RHUBARB

300g brown sugar

1 tsp vanilla essence

1kg rhubarb, washed and chopped

zest and juice of 1 orange

SCONES

225g self-raising flour

pinch of salt

75g butter at room temperature, cubed

40g sugar

1 egg

2 tbsp milk

flour for dusting

1 egg, whisked

sugar for dusting

Melt the sugar and vanilla in a heavy-bottomed saucepan over a gentle heat. Add the rhubarb, orange zest and juice, then cover with a lid and turn the heat up high (this will make the rhubarb fluffy). Cook for about 5 minutes until the rhubarb is soft. Transfer to a baking dish and allow to cool.

To make the scones, sift the flour and salt into a mixing bowl. Add the butter and lightly rub it into the flour, lifting your hands as you work (this will add air to the mixture and make the scones lighter). Mix in the sugar, then make a well in the middle of the bowl.

In a separate bowl gently beat together the egg and milk. Pour into the well in the flour and combine with a palette knife. When it starts to come together, use your hands to finish combining; it should be soft but not sticky. Add more flour if needed to bring the dough together. Turn out onto a floured bench; the dough should come away cleanly from the sides of the bowl.

Form the dough into a long cylindrical shape, then cut into 2cm rounds using a sharp knife.

Preheat the oven to 180°C.

Place the scones on top of the rhubarb so that they cover the fruit but don't overlap.

Glaze with the whisked egg and sprinkle with the sugar. Bake for about 35 minutes until golden brown.

Crêpe Party

Put out plenty of sweet and savoury pancakes along with a range of fillings and let your guests help themselves. If you want to keep it really simple, fresh seasonal fruit is always a winning sweet filling, as is Nutella.

SAVOURY CRÊPE BATTER

250g plain flour

1 tbsp sugar

3 tsp salt

4 eggs

1 egg yolk

100ml cream

650ml milk

½ cup chopped chives

Mix the flour, sugar and salt in an electric mixer on medium speed. Add the eggs and extra yolk, then the cream and milk.

Mix until smooth, turning the mixer up to high speed to make sure there are no lumps of flour. Turn the mixer to medium speed and add the chives. Mix until evenly distributed.

Allow to rest for at least 30 minutes before using.

SWEET CRÊPE BATTER

250g plain flour

2 tbsp sugar

pinch of salt

4 eggs

100ml cream

650ml milk

Mix the flour, sugar and salt in an electric mixer on medium speed. Add the eggs, then the cream and milk. Allow to rest for at least 30 minutes before using.

LEMON CURD FILLING

4 egg yolks

100g castor sugar

50g unsalted butter

zest of 2 lemons

juice of 4 lemons

In a bowl mix together the egg yolks and the sugar, then add the remaining ingredients.

Position the bowl over a saucepan half-filled with water and cook over a medium heat, stirring occasionally.

When the mixture is the same consistency as thickened custard, remove from the heat and pass through a fine sieve. Allow to cool in the fridge before using as a filling for the pancakes.

CHOCOLATE SAUCE FILLING

150ml cream

250g dark chocolate, broken into small pieces

1 tbsp sugar

In a saucepan gently warm the cream over a low heat. Fold in the chocolate and sugar. Remove from the heat when the chocolate has melted.

SEAFOOD FILLING

olive oil

180g prawn meat

10 scallops

10 mussels, steamed and
  cut in half

1 red onion, finely diced

4 cloves garlic, finely diced

250g cherry tomatoes, halved

100ml white wine

200ml tomato juice

2 tbsp capers

extra virgin olive oil

juice of 3 lemons

salt and pepper

small bunch of basil,
  finely chopped

small bunch of chives,
  finely chopped

Heat the olive oil in a frying pan and quickly sear the prawns, scallops and mussels. Remove from the pan and set aside.

In the same pan, cook the onion and garlic until they turn a light golden colour. Add the cherry tomatoes, then the white wine. Cook until reduced by half, then add the tomato juice and reduce by half again.

Add the seafood, capers, a splash of extra virgin olive oil and the lemon juice and warm through. Cook for a further 2–3 minutes. Season with salt and pepper. Just before serving add the chopped herbs and mix well.

PORCINI, CHEESE & HAM FILLING

250ml white wine

50g dried porcini mushrooms

150g Dijon mustard

salt and pepper

50g butter

50g flour

300ml milk

50g Parmesan cheese

250g ham, cut into 5mm cubes

In a saucepan bring the wine to the boil over a medium heat. Add the porcini, turn down the heat and cook slowly until they are very soft and the liquid has reduced by half. If the mushrooms are still firm, top up the wine and cook until soft.

Transfer the mushrooms to a blender or food processor and blend with the Dijon mustard until a smooth paste is formed. Season with salt and pepper.

Gently heat a saucepan and add the butter. Once it is melted, add the flour. In a separate saucepan, bring the milk to the boil, then slowly add it to the butter and flour, mixing continuously until smooth and creamy. Mix in the Parmesan and bring to the boil. Remove from the heat and add the ham, followed by the porcini mixture, a spoonful at a time, stirring until the mixture is smooth and an even tan colour.

METHOD FOR COOKING CRÊPES

Heat a medium-sized non-stick frying pan over a low heat. When reasonably hot, add a little olive oil and pour in about 50ml of pancake batter. Swirl the pan around until the batter has covered the bottom of the pan. Cook for 2 minutes until the mixture has set, flip over with a palette knife or spatula and cook for a further 2–3 minutes.

see photo on pages 8–9

lunch

Lunch is generally a one-plate meal, so whichever dish you decide to serve should look good. 'Big' dishes such as Lancashire hotpot, calamari bolognaise and salmon coulibiac are always excellent choices, not least because they can be placed in the middle of the table along with lots of bread and salad for everyone to help themselves. Light desserts are best; poached fruit is another good option for this time of day.

Salmon Coulibiac

Serves 6

With everything wrapped in the pastry, coulibiac is a meal in itself. It can be made beforehand (up to 24 hours) and kept in the fridge until it's ready to be baked. As it is very filling, you should have plenty left over to eat cold the next day.

100g spinach

salt and pepper

zest and juice of 2 lemons

flour for dusting

500g puff pastry

150g basmati rice, cooked and cooled

400g fresh salmon fillet, boned and skinned

1 tbsp runny honey

50ml extra virgin olive oil

2 tbsp capers

1 tbsp chopped flat-leaf parsley

1 tbsp chopped coriander

2 free-range eggs, hard-boiled, peeled and sliced

2 egg yolks, lightly beaten

lemon wedges to garnish

Preheat the oven to 180°C.

Wilt the spinach in a hot frying pan with plenty of salt and half the lemon juice. Drain well and allow to cool.

On a lightly floured bench roll out the pastry to an A3-sized sheet. Transfer the pastry to an oven tray covered in baking paper.

Place half the wilted spinach lengthways down the middle of the pastry, leaving about 2cm at each end. Spread half the rice over the spinach.

Cut the salmon into 3cm-wide pieces (not too thick so each one cooks through) and season with salt and pepper. Arrange the salmon on top of the rice and drizzle with the honey and olive oil. Sprinkle over the remaining lemon zest and juice, capers, parsley and coriander.

Cover the salmon with slices of egg and spread the remaining rice over the top, followed by a last layer of spinach.

Fold the two short ends of the pastry over and brush with egg yolk. Fold in the two long sides to create a parcel that completely encases the contents. Brush the outside of the parcel with egg yolk.

Bake for 35 minutes. To check if it is cooked, insert a knife into the middle and leave it there for about 20 seconds; if the knife is hot on its removal, then the coulibiac is ready.

Remove from the oven and allow to cool for 5 minutes. Cut the coulibiac into slices and garnish with lemon wedges. Serve warm.

Parma Ham-wrapped Bocconcini with Cannellini Bean Dip

Serves 6

This is a great starter or tapas-style dish, especially if you can get buffalo milk bocconcini. They are soft and juicy and really make a difference. I prefer to use canned cannellini beans – not just because it takes the stress out of cooking them, but in my opinion they're better anyway.

1 white onion, finely chopped
2 cloves garlic, finely chopped
olive oil for frying
1 x 390g can cannellini beans
1 tsp white balsamic vinegar
100ml chicken stock
salt and pepper
100ml extra virgin olive oil
12 bocconcini balls
12 basil leaves
12 slices Parma ham
ciabatta and extra virgin olive oil to serve

In a small saucepan lightly sauté the onion and garlic in the olive oil until soft.

Drain the cannellini beans and wash in a colander to rinse off the brine.

Add the beans, vinegar and chicken stock to the onion and garlic. Bring to the boil and simmer for a few minutes until the beans are soft. Season with salt and pepper.

Place the mixture in a food processor and blend until smooth. With the motor running, slowly drizzle in the extra virgin olive oil.

Transfer the mixture to a bowl, cover with cling film to prevent a skin forming, and keep warm.

Season the bocconcini with salt and pepper. Wrap a basil leaf around each ball, then wrap a slice of Parma ham around to encase.

TO SERVE

Place a couple of spoonfuls of warm bean dip in the middle of each plate and top with two bocconcini balls. Drizzle with extra virgin olive oil and serve with a slice of grilled ciabatta.

Westcoast Whitebait Chowder

Serves 6

Instead of the classic fritter, try this excellent alternative way of serving whitebait. The trick is to make the chowder, then add the whitebait at the end to ensure they don't overcook. I always add a little crème fraîche to round it off and give it a luxurious velvety texture.

1 white onion, chopped

1 leek, finely sliced

1 clove garlic, finely chopped

4 rashers cured pancetta, finely sliced

100g unsalted butter

2 cups dry white wine

3 cups chicken stock

2 cups cream

1 x 410g can corn kernels, drained

1 x 410g can creamed corn

2 large potatoes, peeled and finely diced

fresh whitebait (the quantity depends on how much you like your guests, but don't be stingy)

2 tbsp chopped curly parsley

1 tbsp chopped chives

crème fraîche to garnish

1 tbsp chopped chives

zest of 1 lemon

Slowly sauté the onion, leek, garlic and pancetta in the butter until cooked.

Add the wine and reduce by half, then add the chicken stock and reduce by half again.

Add the cream and both cans of corn. Bring to the boil, add the potatoes and simmer until the potatoes are cooked and the soup has a nice velvety texture.

Just before serving, add the whitebait to the pan and gently simmer for 1–1½ minutes maximum. Stir through the herbs and remove from the heat.

TO SERVE

Ladle the vegetables and whitebait into bowls and pour the soup around them. Garnish with a scoop of crème fraîche mixed with chives and lemon zest.

Lancashire Hotpot

Serves 6

A 'one-pot wonder' that makes good use of a large cast iron-pan. Here, the potatoes trap all the flavour of the lamb – Agria potatoes are best as they hold together nicely, have a great texture and are good at crisping up.

2 carrots, peeled and diced

3 sticks celery, diced

4 cloves garlic, chopped

1 white onion, diced

1 large turnip, diced

1 large swede, diced

100ml olive oil

500g lamb shoulder,
    cut into 12 pieces

1 litre beef stock

3 tomatoes (fresh or tinned
    plum variety), chopped

4 sprigs of fresh thyme

½ cup chopped curly parsley

salt and pepper

4 large Agria potatoes (or any
    other floury variety), peeled

100g butter

Sauté the vegetables in the olive oil until soft. Remove from the pan and set aside.

Using the same pan, sear the lamb on all sides over a high heat until golden brown, about 2–3 minutes. Remove and set aside.

Deglaze the pan with the stock, tomatoes, thyme and parsley. Season with salt and pepper, then bring the mixture to the boil and leave to simmer.

Preheat the oven to 180°C.

Thinly slice the potatoes and toss in a bowl with some salt and pepper.

Arrange the meat evenly in an ovenproof dish. Place the cooked vegetables on top, then make an overlapping layer of potatoes to cover. Pour in the stock mixture to just cover the potatoes.

Cut the butter into cubes or knobs and scatter over the potato layer. Bake for 1 hour, at which point the potatoes should be golden brown.

Cornish Smoked Fish Cakes with Lemon Aïoli

Serves 6

I grew up eating these little beauties. Saffron plays a large part in Cornish food (historically Cornwall regularly traded with Spain: we bought their saffron and they bought our pilchards) and it really makes a difference in this recipe. And while the mayonnaise may seem a strange ingredient in the fish cakes, trust me – it works!

FISH CAKES

zest and juice of 1 lemon

pinch of saffron threads

800g smoked snapper (or any other flaky white fish)

½ cup finely chopped spring onions

2 tbsp wholegrain mustard

1 cup freshly mashed potato

3 tbsp mayonnaise

salt and pepper

1 cup white breadcrumbs

flour for dusting

2 eggs, whisked

butter for frying

lemon halves to garnish

LEMON AÏOLI

100ml lemon juice

100ml white wine vinegar

50g sugar

2 egg yolks

2 tbsp Dijon mustard

500ml olive oil

about 50ml warm water

salt and pepper

Make the fish cakes first. Gently heat the lemon juice in a small saucepan, add the saffron and remove from the heat. Allow to infuse for 15 minutes.

Use your fingers to flake the fish into a bowl. Add the lemon juice and saffron, the spring onions, lemon zest, mustard and potato. Mix well, then add the mayonnaise and season with salt and pepper. If the mixture is too wet, add some breadcrumbs as required.

Divide the mixture into six balls of equal size, flatten each one with the heel of your hand and refrigerate for at least 1 hour.

Make the aïoli while the fish cakes are setting in the fridge. Combine the lemon juice, white wine vinegar and sugar in a saucepan and simmer gently until reduced by half. Allow to cool.

Place the cooled lemon juice mixture in a blender with the egg yolks and mustard. Blend until smooth. With the motor running, slowly add the oil until the mixture is thick. Use a little warm water to thin down the aïoli to the required smooth texture. Season to taste.

Remove the fish cakes from the fridge. Dust them in flour, dip into the whisked eggs and lastly coat with the rest of the breadcrumbs.

Heat some butter in a frying pan until it is foaming. Place the fish cakes in the pan and cook until golden, then turn and cook on the other side.

TO SERVE

The fish cakes will be soft, but that's what makes them nice. They don't need any frills; just some lemon halves on the side and a dollop of lemon aïoli. Add a scoop of spicy potato wedges for a big, filling lunch.

Tiger Prawn, Coconut & Mango Salad

Serves 6

In this light lunchtime salad, perfect for summer, the spiciness of the chilli is mellowed by the creaminess of the coconut and the sweetness of the mango. You could barbecue the prawns instead of poaching them.

18 raw tiger prawns, peeled and deveined

salt and pepper

1 red chilli, deseeded and finely chopped

juice of 3 limes

1 x 400ml can coconut cream

2 tbsp chopped chives

2 tbsp chopped coriander

flaky salt

1 fresh mango

2 tbsp toasted shredded coconut

100g mixed salad leaves

Place the prawns in a saucepan with enough water to cover them. Add a pinch of salt and pepper and bring to the boil. Remove from the heat, drain and allow to cool.

Mix the chilli with the lime juice, then add the coconut cream, chives and coriander. Season with flaky salt. Add the prawns and leave in the fridge to infuse for a couple of hours.

TO SERVE

Lift out the prawns and place them in the centre of a platter and drizzle with the coconut cream dressing. Peel and chop the mango into large dice and sprinkle over the prawns. Garnish with the toasted coconut and salad leaves.

Calamari Bolognaise

Serves 6

A great take on the beef version, using calamari, a cheap seafood. When you mince the calamari it's a good idea to half-freeze it first: it makes it easier to go through the mincer. If you don't have a mincer, cut it into really fine dice.

Spaghetti is the obvious choice of pasta to go with this dish, but I also love it with gnocchi or made into a lasagne.

2 white onions, finely chopped
2 cloves garlic, finely chopped
1 carrot, peeled and chopped
2 sticks celery, finely chopped
50g butter
1 bay leaf
1 cup white wine
6 anchovy fillets, chopped
6 large calamari tubes, minced
1 x 400g can tomatoes, chopped
salt and pepper
600g fresh spaghetti
12 basil leaves, finely chopped
2 tbsp chopped parsley
18 black Kalamata olives, pitted
grated Parmesan cheese
  to serve

Lightly sauté the onions, garlic, carrot and celery in the butter until soft.

Add the bay leaf, wine and anchovies and cook until the wine is reduced by half.

Add the calamari and bring to a simmer, then add the tomatoes. Season with salt and pepper.

Simmer for 30–40 minutes, stirring occasionally.

About 10 minutes before the sauce is ready, cook the spaghetti according to the packet instructions.

Remove the sauce from the heat and add the fresh herbs and olives at the last minute, stirring to combine.

TO SERVE

Add the calamari sauce to the cooked and drained spaghetti. Divide between six bowls and sprinkle with grated Parmesan.

Roast Prune- & Gorgonzola-stuffed Pears with Apple Syrup

Serves 6

Try this recipe in late autumn when pears are in season, either as an easy starter or a main course for lunch. The apple syrup is a must; it contrasts so well with the sweet prunes and tangy blue cheese.

STUFFED PEARS

6 ripe pears

100g pitted prunes, chopped

50g toasted walnuts, chopped

60ml brandy

100g Gorgonzola cheese, crumbled

salt and pepper

2 cups white wine

3 tbsp clear honey

zest and juice of 1 lemon

APPLE SYRUP

500ml clear apple juice

1 cinnamon stick

100g castor sugar

zest of 1 lemon

Preheat the oven to 160°C.

Carefully peel the pears, leaving the stems attached. Halve and remove the cores using a small paring knife.

Mix together the prunes, walnuts, brandy and Gorgonzola in a bowl. Season with salt and pepper, then stuff the pears with this mixture. Arrange the pears so they stand upright in a baking dish.

Mix together the wine, honey, lemon zest and juice, and pour over the pears.

Bake for 45 minutes or until the pears are soft.

To make the syrup, combine all the ingredients in a stainless steel saucepan and simmer until reduced to a sticky glaze. Pass the syrup through a sieve and allow to cool in the fridge.

TO SERVE

Place the pears on a serving platter and drizzle with the apple syrup. Serve warm with a crunchy salad and toasted bread.

Apple Donuts with Five-spice Custards

Serves 6

For a scrumptious lunchtime treat, these little custards are fantastic spooned onto the donuts. Or you can just dip the donuts straight into the custard.

DONUTS
60g unsalted butter
1 cup boiling hot milk
⅓ cup sugar
½ tsp salt
1 tbsp active dried yeast
pinch of nutmeg
2 eggs, beaten
3½ cups sifted plain flour
2 apples, peeled and grated
canola oil for deep-frying
cinnamon sugar to serve

FIVE-SPICE CUSTARDS
1 litre cream
12 egg yolks
150g sugar
1 tsp Chinese five-spice powder
1 tbsp vanilla essence

To make the donuts, melt the butter in the hot milk, add 1 tsp of sugar and the salt. Allow to cool.

Beat in the yeast, nutmeg, eggs, the remaining sugar and half the flour. Add the rest of the flour to form a sticky dough. Fold in the grated apple.

Turn out the dough onto a floured bench and knead for 5 minutes. Leave in a warm place for 1–1½ hours to rise.

Roll out the dough to 5mm deep. Using a pastry cutter, cut out about 18 circles. If you prefer donut rings to balls, remove the centre of each circle. Allow to rise for a further 30–45 minutes.

Heat the oil to 365°C and fry the donuts, a few at a time, for 1–2 minutes on each side or until brown. Drain on kitchen paper and keep warm.

Preheat the oven to 90°C. Heat the cream for the custards in a saucepan to just under boiling point, about 80°C.

Combine the egg yolks, sugar, five-spice powder and vanilla essence in a large mixing bowl and whisk until light and fluffy.

Slowly add the hot cream to the egg mixture, making sure the mixture doesn't split.

Allow the mixture to settle for about 10 minutes, skimming off any bubbles that form on the top.

Pour the custard into six individual moulds and bake in a water bath for about 25–30 minutes until set.

TO SERVE
Dust the donuts with cinnamon sugar and serve with the custards.

Poached White Peaches with Mint & Beaumes de Venise

Serves 6

A fragrant light dessert for late summer when peaches are at their best. As peaches will keep in the fridge for a few days, you can poach a few extra to indulge in later.

6 fresh white peaches
375ml bottle Beaumes de Venise
  (or dessert wine of your choice)
zest of 1 lemon
50g icing sugar, sifted
1 cup mascarpone
15 mint leaves, finely sliced
biscotti or amaretti biscuits
  to serve

Blanch the peaches in boiling water for 10–15 seconds until the skin starts to peel off. Plunge them into ice-cold water, then drain on kitchen paper before removing any skin that may still be attached. Cut the peaches in half and remove the stones.

Pour the wine into a saucepan and bring to a simmer over a medium heat. Place the peaches in the wine and simmer for about 5 minutes until soft. Using a slotted spoon, remove the peaches and refrigerate to chill. Reserve the wine.

Mix together the lemon zest, sifted icing sugar and mascarpone. Set aside until required.

TO SERVE

Place the poached peach halves in a serving dish, pour the wine over them and sprinkle with the mint. At the table, place a generous spoonful of the mascarpone mixture on each peach and serve with biscotti or amaretti biscuits on the side.

Red Wine-poached Pears with Date & Walnut Crème Fraîche

Serves 6

In this recipe the pears are served warm, but they're also fantastic cold (try them with a nice blue cheese). Keep them for up to two weeks in the fridge in an airtight container filled to the top with the poaching liquid and all air bubbles removed.

POACHED PEARS

6 unripe pears

1 litre full-bodied red wine, e.g. shiraz or cabernet sauvignon

1 cinnamon stick

2 cloves

2 star anise

2 cups sugar

DATE & WALNUT CRÈME FRAÎCHE

2 cups crème fraîche

½ cup chopped pitted dates

½ cup chopped toasted walnuts

2 tbsp clear honey

30ml dark rum

Peel the pears, leaving them whole with the stems attached.

Combine all the remaining ingredients in a saucepan and bring to the boil.

When the wine mixture reaches boiling point, add the pears. Cover and gently simmer for about 30 minutes until the pears have softened; they should be firm but easy to cut with a knife.

Gently remove the pears from the liquid and allow both pears and liquid to cool. Once cool, return the pears to the liquid and leave to marinate for 30 minutes.

Combine all the ingredients for the crème fraîche and allow to set in the fridge for 30 minutes.

TO SERVE

Place a pear in the middle of each serving bowl and place a spoonful of the crème fraîche alongside. Gently pour some poaching liquid around each pear.

afternoon tea

Cooking for this part of the day has special meaning for me as my first job in London at a big hotel involved making hundreds of afternoon tea sandwiches to accompany an array of dainty pastries and cakes.

In this chapter I've deliberately left out classic scones, but added instead a recipe for drop scones which are a wonderful alternative. There are no rules for what to serve for afternoon tea; it's about the occasion itself and, of course, a good-quality cup of leaf tea.

Date & Sultana Loaf

Serves 6

More a light fruitcake, this is very good toasted or spread with butter and eaten fresh.

butter for greasing
4 eggs
150g castor sugar
100g sultanas
100 dates, pitted and chopped
70g mixed peel
50g glacé cherries, chopped
90ml cherry brandy
200ml dessert wine
350g flour
5 tsp baking powder
zest of 1 lemon

Preheat the oven to 180°C.

Grease a loaf tin with butter and place in the fridge so the butter sets.

In a large bowl cream the eggs and sugar until light and fluffy. Fold in the dried fruit, then add the brandy and wine. Fold in the flour, baking powder and lemon zest, then allow the mixture to rest for 15 minutes. Pour into the prepared loaf tin and bake for 1 hour. The loaf is cooked when a small sharp knife is inserted into the centre and comes out clean.

Remove from the oven and allow to cool on a cake wire.

Cherry Clafoutis

Serves 10

A favourite of mine in summer when cherries are in season, these tarts are simple to make and are all about allowing fresh cherries to strut their stuff.

500g sweet shortcrust pastry
500ml cream
8 egg yolks
100g castor sugar
½ tsp almond essence
½ cup almonds, toasted
  and ground
30 fresh cherries, pitted

Preheat the oven to 150°C.

Grease 10 small (10cm) tart tins. Divide the pastry into 10 portions and line each tin evenly. Line the pastry with baking paper and fill with baking beans. Bake for 10–15 minutes or until golden and cooked through, then allow to cool.

In a small saucepan heat the cream to just under boiling point, then remove from the heat. In a large bowl combine the egg yolks, sugar and almond essence and whisk until pale. Slowly and carefully add the hot cream to the egg mixture, bit by bit, making sure not to cook the eggs in the process. Add the ground almonds and mix to combine.

Divide the cherries between the tart tins, then pour in enough custard to cover. Bake at 150°C for 20–25 minutes or until the custard has set (although it should still wobble a bit in the middle as it will continue to cook once out of the oven).

Date & Sultana Loaf

Crumpets

Serves 6

Once you've mastered these crumpets you'll never buy the supermarket ones again. Light and fluffy, they are an ideal afternoon tea treat served with your favourite topping.

450g plain flour, sifted
½ tsp salt
1 tsp castor sugar
10g fresh yeast
300ml warm milk
300ml warm water
canola oil

4 x 7.5cm crumpet rings

crème fraîche and jam to serve

Place the flour and salt in a large bowl. Stir in the sugar and yeast, making a well in the centre. Pour in the warm milk and water, mixing to form a thick batter, then beat well until completely combined.

Cover with a tea towel or cling film and leave in a warm place for about 1 hour until the batter takes on a light spongy texture. Stir well to knock out any air bubbles, then pour into a large jug.

Thoroughly grease four 7.5cm crumpet rings.

Heat a little oil in a large non-stick frying pan over a very low heat. Wipe out the pan with some kitchen paper to remove any excess oil. Place the greased crumpet rings in the pan and leave to heat for 2–3 minutes.

Pour in enough mixture to fill the rings just over halfway up the side of each. Leave to cook until a number of small holes appear on the surface and the batter is just starting to dry out, about 8–10 minutes.

Remove the rings, leaving the crumpets in the pan. Turn over to cook for 1–2 minutes on the other side. Place the first batch on a wire rack and keep warm while you cook the remaining mixture.

TO SERVE

Serve with crème fraîche and jam or your choice of condiment.

Bakewell Tart

Serves 6

A real English classic, which in my opinion can more than match any other tart.

SWEET PASTRY

300g plain flour, plus extra
   for dusting
125g unsalted butter
30g castor sugar
1 egg
2 tbsp milk to bind if required
1 egg, beaten

FRANGIPANE

225g unsalted soft butter
225g castor sugar
225g ground almonds
3 large eggs
zest of 1 lemon
50g plain flour

100g of your favourite
   raspberry jam
50g flaked almonds

Make the pastry first. Place the flour, butter, sugar and egg into a food processor and pulse to combine. If necessary, add a little milk to help bring the mixture together. Turn out the dough onto a floured bench and roll out until large enough to line a greased 26cm tart tin. Carefully lift the pastry into the tin and refrigerate for 1 hour.

Preheat the oven to 200°C. Line the chilled pastry shell with a sheet of greaseproof paper weighed down with baking beans or rice, then bake for 15–20 minutes.

Remove the paper and beans from the shell and brush the pastry with the beaten egg. Return to the oven for a further 5 minutes until golden brown. Remove from the oven and reduce the oven temperature to 180°C. Leave the pastry shell to cool.

To make the frangipane, cream the butter and sugar in a bowl until light and fluffy. Mix in the ground almonds then crack in the eggs, one at a time, beating well between each addition (don't worry if the mixture begins to split; just add a little of the flour). Fold in the lemon zest and the flour.

Spread the jam across the base of the pastry shell, leaving a 1cm gap around the edge. Spread the frangipane over the jam and sprinkle with the flaked almonds.

Bake for 20 minutes. Allow to cool before cutting into wedges and serving with pouring cream or Greek yoghurt.

see photo on pages 44–45

Cornish Saffron Cake

Serves 6

You see these cakes, which remind me of Italian panettone, in bakeries all over Cornwall. They are a bit like Cornish pasties in that every baker and housewife has their own version. I find the best place to buy fresh yeast is from your local baker who should be happy to sell you some.

pinch of saffron threads
100ml warm milk
45g fresh yeast
120g castor sugar
675g plain flour
pinch of nutmeg
6 eggs
450g salted butter, softened and cut into small chunks
450g currants
zest of 3 lemons

Put the saffron into a bowl, add the warm milk and refrigerate overnight.

Preheat the oven to 180°C.

Bring the milk to room temperature. Mix in the yeast and stir until dissolved.

Place the sugar, flour and nutmeg in the bowl of a mixer and mix for 1 minute. Add the milk mixture and mix until smooth. Add the eggs, one at a time, and mix until smooth. Add the butter, a little at a time, and continue to mix until smooth again. Add the currants and lemon zest, lower the speed to slow and mix for 2 minutes.

Turn out the dough and divide into four pieces of equal size. Roll each piece into a smooth ball.

Grease two loaf tins and place two dough balls in each tin. Leave to rise in a warm oven or similarly warm place until doubled in size, about 1 hour.

Bake for 45 minutes, then turn out onto a wire rack to cool.

Serve cut into slices at least half an inch thick and spread with butter or with a dollop of clotted cream.

Cinnamon Drop Scones with Blueberry Cream

Serves 6

As my mother was always baking, we often had scones – these drop scones were the ones we'd ask for most and, like my mother, you can experiment and add fruit to the recipe if you like.

DROP SCONES

225g self-raising flour
½ tsp mixed spice
1 tbsp ground cinnamon
55g castor sugar
1 tbsp runny honey
2 eggs, beaten
300ml milk
oil for cooking
icing sugar for dusting

BLUEBERRY CREAM

1 punnet blueberries
75g icing sugar
30ml dark rum
zest of 1 lemon
500ml cream, whipped

Place the flour, mixed spice, cinnamon and sugar in a bowl, making a well in the centre.

Mix together the honey and egg and pour into the well. Gradually add the milk, beating until smooth.

Lightly grease a heavy-bottomed frying pan or griddle with the oil and heat until moderately hot. Drop a tablespoonful of the mixture, several at a time, into the pan and cook until bubbles appear on the surface and the underneath of each is golden brown. Turn over and cook on the other side for 1–2 minutes.

Place the hot scones between the folds of a clean tea towel or layers of kitchen paper and keep warm. Repeat until all the batter is used.

Mix the blueberries with the icing sugar and rum, and leave for 30 minutes to infuse.

Add the lemon zest to the berries and fold in the whipped cream. Check for sweetness and add more icing sugar if desired.

TO SERVE

Dust the warm drop scones with icing sugar and serve with dollops of blueberry cream.

Baklava Fingers with Lemon Crème Fraîche

Serves 6

I have made this traditional Middle Eastern dessert in easy-to-handle cigar shapes, rather than the usual large 'family size' tray. Made like this, baklava can also serve as a great pass-around dessert with the crème fraîche as a dipping sauce.

BAKLAVA

90g walnuts, chopped
90g pecans, chopped
60g pistachio nuts, chopped
90g hazelnuts, chopped
60g almonds, chopped
1 tsp ground cinnamon
90g ground almonds
zest of 1 lemon
100g runny honey
1 packet filo pastry
1 egg, beaten
60g unsalted butter, melted

LEMON CRÈME FRAÎCHE

500ml crème fraîche
60g candied lemon, chopped
60ml limoncello liqueur
90g icing sugar

Preheat the oven to 180°C.

Place all the chopped nuts in a roasting dish and roast for about 5 minutes until lightly golden. Remove the dish from the oven and stir in the cinnamon, ground almonds, lemon zest and honey. Mix well to form a nice moist paste, adding a little more honey if a wetter consistency is desired.

Cut the filo pastry into 15cm squares. Place one piece of filo on top of another to create a double layer, then brush all over with the beaten egg. Place a generous spoonful of nut mixture in the centre of the filo square, then fold in two sides to meet in the middle. Roll up the filo starting from one of the shorter, open ends to achieve a cigar shape. Repeat with the rest of the filo to use up all the nut mixture.

Place the cigar shapes in the fridge for 30 minutes to set.

When ready to bake, brush each filo finger with some of the melted butter and place on a baking tray. Bake at 180°C for 20 minutes until golden brown and crisp.

While the filo fingers are baking, prepare the lemon crème fraîche. Combine all the ingredients in a mixing bowl and gently fold together. Refrigerate until needed.

Remove the filo fingers from the oven and brush with the remaining butter. Serve hot with the lemon crème fraîche.

Classic Fruitcake

Serves 6

This recipe is incredibly moist and keeps for six months when sealed in an airtight container. The secret, which I learnt from my mum when I was very young, is to soak the fruit in hot tea overnight to make it moist.

700g sultanas

200g currants

200g raisins

100g dates, chopped

100g figs, chopped

50g red glacé cherries

50g green glacé cherries

100g glacé ginger, chopped

100g mixed peel, chopped

1 litre English breakfast tea

100ml sweet sherry

100ml brandy

100ml dark rum

2 tsp vanilla essence

2 tsp almond essence

300g salted butter

200g brown sugar

8 eggs

1 tsp mixed spice

1½ tsp cinnamon powder

¼ tsp ground cloves

600g all-purpose flour

140g whole almonds

200g walnut halves

extra almonds and glacé cherries for topping

icing sugar to garnish

Combine the fruit in a bowl, pour over the hot tea and leave overnight.

The next day, drain off the tea and pour over the sherry, brandy, rum, vanilla essence and almond essence. Mix well.

Pre-heat the oven to 160°C.

Cream the butter and sugar just enough to get rid of any lumps. Add the eggs one by one, continuing to mix while adding them. Add the spices and fold in the flour.

Fold in the almonds, walnuts and fruit mixture and mix well. Allow to rest for 30 minutes.

Grease six small loaf tins or one 26cm baking tin. Spoon cake mixture into tins and top with extra almonds and glacé cherries.

Bake for 45 minutes, then lower the temperature to 120°C and bake for a further hour. Test to see if it is ready by inserting a thin knife into the middle of the cake. If the mixture sticks to the knife, further baking is required.

Remove and allow to cool before serving.

TO SERVE

Slice into small pieces and dust with icing sugar.

barbecue

Barbecues offer the perfect opportunity to have a bit of fun with entertaining, but keep in mind that barbecue doesn't mean that everything should taste of charcoal – in other words, take care to avoid burning the food.

For flavour, there's nothing like cooking over charcoal. It's a bit more work, but the end result will be worth it. Another great way to add flavour is to use marinades. A good overnight soak in one of the recommended brews is sure to rev up your cut of meat.

Sage, Onion and Garlic Brioche

Makes 4 x 20cm rounds

It's a myth that brioche is hard to make, as this foolproof recipe verifies. Leaving the dough to prove overnight allows the butter to set before it is rolled out the next day.

BRIOCHE
25g active dried yeast
50ml warm water
1kg all-purpose flour
12 eggs
30g sugar
25g salt
600g unsalted butter, softened
canola oil for greasing

ONION & GARLIC MIX
100ml olive oil
4 red onions, finely sliced
10 cloves garlic, finely sliced
bunch of sage, roughly chopped
salt and pepper

Place the yeast in the warm water and leave to activate for about 5 minutes.

Combine the flour, eggs, sugar, salt and yeast/water mix in the bowl of a mixer. Mix for about 3 minutes on a low speed until well combined. Slowly add the butter, about 100g at a time. Mix again on a low speed for another 10 minutes. Cover with cling film and refrigerate overnight.

Heat the oil in a heavy-based frying pan or saucepan and slowly cook the onion and garlic until soft without browning. Add the sage and season to taste. Allow to cool.

Preheat the oven to 200°C. Divide the dough into four equal pieces and roll out each piece to fit a 20cm-diameter baking tin that has been brushed with canola oil.

Spread a thin layer of the onion and garlic mix over each brioche and bake for 20–25 minutes until golden.

New Potatoes Baked 'en Papillote' with Lemon & Rosemary

Serves 6

Eduardo, a Portuguese kitchenhand with whom I worked in London, showed me how to make this dish, but I've since added a few ingredients. Like anything cooked in a bag, you get a lot of flavour sealed in.

500g Jersey Bennes or waxy new potatoes of your choice, washed

zest and juice of 1 lemon

leaves from 1 sprig of rosemary

½ red chilli, deseeded and finely chopped

100ml extra virgin olive oil

3 cloves garlic, finely chopped

1 red onion, finely chopped

pinch of smoked paprika

salt and pepper

75g Fontina cheese, grated

Combine the first eight ingredients in a bowl and season well with salt and pepper.

Lay out a large sheet of tinfoil on the bench and arrange the potatoes on it. Gather together the edges of the tinfoil to seal in the potatoes.

Place on a barbecue hotplate and cook slowly, keeping the tinfoil sealed for about 1 hour or until the potatoes are cooked through.

Serve with the grated cheese on top.

Butterfly Lamb Shoulder with Provençal Crust

Serves 6

This Provençal recipe uses a kind of sloppy tapenade to marinate the lamb. To keep the meat moist, baste it as often as possible with the marinade during cooking.

MARINADE

1 cup Kalamata olives, pitted

4 anchovy fillets

leaves from 1 sprig of rosemary

¼ cup olive oil

1 tbsp capers

2 cloves garlic

cracked pepper to taste

zest and juice of 1 lemon

1 lamb shoulder, boned

To make the marinade, place all the ingredients except the lemon juice and zest in a food processor and blend until smooth. Remove from the processor and add the zest and juice to the mixture. Stir to combine.

Marinate the lamb in the mixture for at least 2–3 hours before cooking. Cook the lamb slowly on the barbecue hotplate for about 1½ hours, turning and basting regularly. Keep the lamb covered with the hood, if you have one, throughout. Alternatively, cover the lamb with tinfoil to keep the heat in.

Barbecued Cockles Casino

Serves 6

You can make this succulent little dish with clams or cockles – it's an ideal appetiser for passing around before the main event.

6 slices pancetta or streaky bacon, finely chopped

50ml extra virgin olive oil

½ red onion, finely chopped

1 clove garlic, finely chopped

½ red capsicum (pepper), finely diced

½ tsp freshly chopped thyme

zest and juice of 1 lemon

1 tsp white balsamic vinegar

50g freshly grated Parmesan cheese

salt and pepper

rock salt

24 large cockles with tops shucked (ask the fishmonger to do this)

lemon wedges to garnish

Cook the pancetta in some of the olive oil over a moderate heat in a non-stick frying pan until it caramelises, then transfer it with a slotted spoon to drain on kitchen paper.

In the same pan cook the onion and garlic in the oil over a moderately low heat until softened. Add the capsicum, thyme, lemon zest and juice, and cook until the capsicum is tender.

Transfer the mixture to a small bowl and stir in the pancetta, vinegar, Parmesan and salt and pepper to taste. Allow to cool in the fridge.

Cover a skillet with rock salt and arrange the cockles on top – the salt will stop them slipping around. Top each cockle with a spoonful of the capsicum mixture.

Place the skillet on the barbecue grill and cover with an ovenproof bowl (or pull down the hood if your barbecue has one). Cook over a high heat for 15 minutes until the cockles are cooked and the topping is golden brown.

TO SERVE
Remove the cockles from the skillet and transfer to a serving platter. Garnish with the lemon wedges and serve immediately.

Baked Sweetcorn with Anchovy & Smoked Paprika Butter

Serves 6

Another favourite in my household, this very cheap and easy-to-put-together combination makes a great accompaniment to barbecued lamb or steak. The salty anchovies provide a good contrast to the sweetness of the corn and the smokiness of the paprika.

I recommend cutting the corn into 3–4cm discs after cooking to make them easy to eat.

150g butter
75ml extra virgin olive oil
6 anchovy fillets
4 tbsp white balsamic vinegar
½ tsp smoked paprika
1 clove garlic, chopped
2 tbsp chopped flat-leaf parsley
6 fresh corn cobs, shucked
salt and pepper

Blend the butter, olive oil and anchovies in a food processor.

Heat the balsamic vinegar and paprika in a small saucepan until the liquid boils. Allow to cool, then stir in the butter mixture. Transfer to a bowl and add the garlic and parsley.

Place each corn cob on a piece of tinfoil large enough to completely enclose the corn. Season with salt and pepper, then spread the butter mix over the corn. Fold the tinfoil around each corn cob to seal, and cook on the hotplate (not the grill, or the corn will burn) before you start cooking the rest of the meal. As long as you don't remove the tinfoil, the corn will stay moist. Whole cobs take about 10–15 minutes to cook.

TO SERVE

Carefully remove the tinfoil; there'll be hot buttery juice under the corn. Pour the juice over the corn and on whatever else you're grilling – it goes wonderfully with everything!

Chicken & Lime Pockets with Sweet & Sour Sauce

Serves 6

These little pockets are packed with simple flavours that are perfect for a barbecue. Because they are wrapped in tinfoil, they will stay really moist during the cooking process.

2 tsp olive oil

6 skinless and boneless
  chicken breasts

salt and pepper

2 tbsp miso paste

zest and juice of 1 lime

2 tbsp soy sauce

6 radishes, grated

2 cloves garlic, finely sliced

12 lime slices

SWEET & SOUR SAUCE

2 tbsp soy sauce

2 tbsp olive oil

juice of 1 lime

salt and pepper

1 tbsp runny honey

pinch of chilli powder

2 spring onions, finely chopped

1 tbsp toasted sesame seeds

Cut out 12 squares of tinfoil, each about 15cm in size, and drizzle one side with a little olive oil.

Thinly slice each chicken breast to make eight slices and season them with salt and pepper. Place four slices of chicken on the centre of each piece of foil.

Mix together the miso paste, lime zest and juice, and soy sauce, then pour it over the chicken slices. Sprinkle with the radishes and garlic, and top with a slice of lime.

Fold the foil to make a flat parcel, folding in the edges to seal. Barbecue over a medium heat until steam starts to come out of the pockets, then cook for a further 3–4 minutes. The chicken should be cooked through after this time but open one of the parcels to check.

To make the dressing, combine all the ingredients in a bowl or jar and mix well.

TO SERVE

Let your guests open the pockets themselves and serve the sweet & sour sauce on the side.

Grilled Chicken & Red Curry Sandwiches with Banana Chutney

Serves 6

I love the spicy sweet chutney that goes with this spicy chicken sandwich and often make more than I need because it keeps well in the fridge for a couple of weeks.

MARINATED CHICKEN

2 tsp red curry paste

zest and juice of 2 limes

salt and pepper

1 tbsp chopped coriander

1 tbsp chopped mint

6 boneless chicken breasts

BANANA CHUTNEY

1 white onion, finely chopped

3 cloves garlic, finely chopped

50ml canola oil

½ medium-sized red chilli,
   deseeded and finely chopped

½ tsp smoked paprika

1 tsp ground ginger

100g brown sugar

100ml white wine vinegar

80g sultanas

zest of 1 lemon

6 firm bananas, peeled
   and chopped

2 tbsp chopped coriander

salt and pepper

SANDWICH

grilled ciabatta bread

coriander and mint leaves

lime juice

Mix together all the marinade ingredients in a bowl with the chicken and leave to marinate for 2 hours in the fridge.

Barbecue the chicken over a medium heat until it is cooked through and tender, and the skin is crisp.

Make the chutney while the chicken is marinating. Fry the onion and garlic in the oil until soft. Add the chilli, smoked paprika and ginger and cook for a further 2–3 minutes over a low heat.

Add the brown sugar and vinegar and bring to the boil. Simmer until reduced to a syrup.

Add the sultanas and lemon zest and cook for 2–3 minutes.

Remove from the heat and fold in the chopped banana. Return to the heat and cook until the banana is soft, but not mushy.

Fold in the coriander, season with salt and pepper, and allow to cool.

TO SERVE

Slice the cooked chicken breast and place on the grilled ciabatta. Top with some coriander and mint, a squeeze of fresh lime and a scoop of the banana chutney.

Spiced Whole Pork Belly with Crispy Courgette & Orange Salad

Serves 6

The trick here is to poach the pork belly first so you cut down the time on the barbecue, which can dry it out. The belly can take a lot of spice, but the sweet orange salad complements this beautifully.

Buy the pork from your butcher – who will cut it to size and remove the bones.

1kg pork belly, skin on

1 tbsp runny honey

2 tbsp hoisin sauce

MARINADE

3 star anise

3 cloves

½ tsp chilli flakes

1 cup white sugar

2 tbsp white wine vinegar

12 coriander seeds

SALAD

3 courgettes (zucchini)

salt and pepper

olive oil for cooking

2 oranges

50ml extra virgin olive oil for salad dressing

3 tbsp toasted pine nuts

3 tbsp toasted peanuts

12 mint leaves

Preheat the oven to 160°C. Place the pork belly skin-side up in a deep braising dish and cover with cold water. Add the marinade ingredients to the dish and cover with tinfoil. Cook for 1½ hours.

Remove the meat and allow to cool in the fridge. Transfer the cooking liquid to a saucepan and reduce until it forms a syrupy glaze. Remove from the heat and mix in the honey and hoisin sauce. Set aside until required.

Using your fingers, peel the skin off the pork belly. Place the skin on an oven tray and bake at 180°C for 10–15 minutes or until crispy.

Slice the courgettes lengthways into thin strips. Toss in a bowl along with salt, pepper and olive oil and cook on the barbecue grill until golden and crispy. Set aside on kitchen paper to drain.

Place pork on the barbecue hotplate. Cook until tender, about 20–30 minutes, brushing with the hoisin glaze as it cooks.

Peel and segment the oranges for the salad. Squeeze the segments and mix the resulting juice with the extra virgin olive oil to make a dressing. Mix together the orange segments with the crispy courgettes, nuts and mint leaves and toss with the dressing.

TO SERVE

Place the courgette and orange salad in the middle of a platter. Slice the belly into thick steaks and arrange around the salad. Using a pair of scissors, cut the pork crackling and arrange on top of the pork.

Paua Burgers with Thousand Island Dressing

Serves 6

I love paua (abalone) fritters, especially this recipe, which I've jazzed up with some Asian flavours and a classic Thousand Island dressing. Buy good quality burger buns or, better still, make your own bread rolls.

PAUA

4 large paua (abalone), minced

150g white breadcrumbs

2 large eggs

½ cup coconut cream

1 tsp fish sauce

zest and juice of 1 lime

½ red chilli, deseeded and finely chopped

½ tsp sesame oil

salt and pepper

2 spring onions, finely chopped

THOUSAND ISLAND DRESSING

2 egg yolks

2 tbsp Dijon mustard

2 tbsp white wine vinegar

salt and pepper

250ml extra virgin olive oil

½ cup tomato sauce

4 tbsp Worcestershire sauce

4 tbsp horseradish cream

Tabasco sauce to taste

BURGERS

6 burger buns

juice of 1 lemon

3 tomatoes, sliced

crunchy iceberg lettuce leaves

Mix together the paua and breadcrumbs. Add the eggs and coconut cream and mix to form a firm patty-like mixture. If it's too wet, add a few more breadcrumbs.

Fold in the remaining ingredients and refrigerate to set for about 2 hours before dividing the mixture into six equal portions.

Grill on the barbecue until crisp on the outside but moist on the inside.

To make the dressing, blend the egg yolks, mustard, vinegar, salt and pepper in a food processor until light and fluffy. With the motor running, slowly add the oil until the mixture thickens. Add the tomato sauce, Worcestershire sauce and horseradish cream and mix to combine. Add the Tabasco and season to taste.

Split and toast the buns. Place a cooked paua patty on each base. Squeeze on some lemon juice, add some slices of tomato, lettuce leaves and a spoonful of the dressing, then top with the other half of the bun.

Spatchcock Chicken with Green Olives & Citrus Fruit

Serves 6

The best and cheapest way to cook chicken on a barbecue is simply to cook it whole. The term spatchcock means to cut out the backbone so that the chicken can be spread flat before grilling.

1 medium free-range chicken

olive oil

salt and pepper

1 red onion, sliced

1 orange, peeled and cut into segments

1 grapefruit, peeled and cut into segments

1 lemon, peeled and cut into segments

1 lime, peeled and cut into segments

18 large green olives

1 clove garlic, finely chopped

1 cup diced watermelon

2 tbsp chopped flat-leaf parsley

2 tbsp chopped coriander

100ml extra virgin olive oil

100g feta cheese, diced

Cut and remove the backbone from the chicken so that it can lie flat. Rub the skin with the oil and season with salt and pepper.

Place the chicken on the barbecue grill skin side up and cook over a medium heat for 10 minutes. Turn over and cook the other side for a further 10 minutes until golden. Repeat this process for both sides.

Transfer the cooked chicken to a chopping board and cut off the legs. Cut each leg in half by separating the thigh from the drumstick. Cut the breast down the middle and divide into six pieces.

TO SERVE

Place the chicken pieces in a large bowl and add the rest of the ingredients except the feta. Gently toss to combine, transfer to a serving platter, then sprinkle with the diced feta and serve.

Venison Koftas with Mint & Yoghurt Dressing

Serves 6

While lamb usually features in Middle-Eastern dishes, this venison version is low in fat, high in flavour and great for barbecues. And the mint and yoghurt are perfect cool partners. Make sure the grill is really hot in order to get the best flavour from the venison.

KOFTAS

500g venison mince

1 onion, chopped and cooked until soft

4 cloves garlic, chopped and cooked until soft

1 egg

1 egg yolk

100g ground almonds

pinch of chilli powder

pinch of smoked sweet paprika

1 red chilli, deseeded and chopped

1 tbsp thick pomegranate syrup

50g Parmesan cheese, grated

salt and pepper

12 bamboo kebab skewers, soaked in water for at least 30 minutes

oil for cooking

YOGHURT DRESSING

1 cup natural thick yoghurt

2 tbsp chopped mint

1 tbsp runny honey

juice of 1 lemon

salt and pepper

Thoroughly mix all the ingredients for the koftas in the bowl of a mixer.

Divide the mixture into 12 equal portions, roll into balls and refrigerate for 30 minutes.

Remove from the fridge and roll each ball into a longish rugby ball shape.

Fit one kofta on each bamboo skewer, brush with oil and grill on the barbecue until charred on each side, about 2 minutes.

Combine all the ingredients for the dressing and mix well.

Serve the koftas warm with the yoghurt dressing on the side.

Grilled Sicilian Caponata

Serves 6

This tasty vegetable dish is a great accompaniment to barbecued food in the summer when capsicums are plentiful and cheap. Cook the capsicums three-quarters through so they keep a bit of crunch.

2 medium aubergines
   (eggplants), cut into 2cm cubes

salt

3–4 tbsp extra virgin olive oil,
   plus extra for drizzling

1 red onion, finely chopped

1 white onion, finely chopped

2 courgettes (zucchini),
   cut into 2cm cubes

2 celery sticks, roughly chopped

2 red capsicums (peppers),
   deseeded and chopped

flaky sea salt and freshly ground
   black pepper

100g green olives, pitted and
   cut in half

3 tbsp small capers, drained
   and chopped

30ml white balsamic vinegar

1 tbsp castor sugar

2 tbsp roughly chopped parsley

Sprinkle the cubed aubergines with salt and leave to drain in a colander for 30 minutes.

Heat some of the olive oil on the barbecue hotplate and cook the aubergines over a moderate heat for 10 minutes until golden brown and cooked through. When cooked, set aside and allow to cool to room temperature.

Heat the remaining olive oil on the hotplate and cook the onions along with the courgettes, celery and capsicums. Season with flaky sea salt and freshly ground black pepper. Add the olives and cook for 5 minutes.

Place the cooled aubergines and the capers in a large bowl and add the white balsamic vinegar and sugar. Add the grilled vegetables to the bowl while they are hot. Add the parsley and mix together.

Drizzle with extra virgin olive oil and serve either hot or cold.

Marinades

Marinating meat is a great way of pepping up the flavour, especially before barbecuing or grilling. In most cases it's best to leave the marinade on the meat for 24 hours before cooking, although take care when marinating seafood as salt from the marinade can sometimes draw out too much moisture, leaving seafood dry. If you put the meat into a plastic bag, then pour in the marinade, you can really work in the marinade without getting your hands dirty. It also seals in the spices and ensures the marinade stays in contact with the meat a lot better than if it's done in a dish.

Another good thing about marinades is that they can be made in advance and will keep for a week or two in the fridge.

The best way to make these recipes is to combine all the ingredients in a liquidiser or blender.

POULTRY

LEMON & SAGE MARINADE

3 cloves garlic

zest and juice of 2 lemons

¼ cup sage leaves

½ cup curly parsley

¼ cup olive oil

1 tbsp salt

½ tbsp cracked pepper

GARLIC CAJUN MARINADE

6 cloves garlic

1 cup olive oil

½ bunch of coriander

1 onion

2 tbsp red wine vinegar

1 tbsp Cajun spice

LAMB

MEDITERRANEAN MARINADE

50g black olives, pitted

½ red chilli

4 cloves garlic

6 anchovy fillets

½ cup rosemary leaves

½ cup curly parsley leaves

½ cup olive oil

1 tbsp salt

1 tsp cracked pepper

SPICY MOROCCAN MARINADE

¼ cup olive oil

1 large onion

6 cloves garlic

1 tsp chilli powder

1 tsp ground cumin

1 tsp ground coriander

1 tsp ground turmeric

1 tsp smoked paprika

BEEF

WHOLEGRAIN MUSTARD & ONION MARINADE

2 tbsp wholegrain mustard

1 onion

4 cloves garlic

1 tbsp dried sage

1 tbsp white wine vinegar

½ cup olive oil

½ red chilli, deseeded

BLACK BEER & PEPPER MARINADE

1 x 330ml bottle black beer

1 tbsp cracked pepper

½ cup canola oil

1 onion

4 cloves garlic

1 tsp English mustard

1 cup curly parsley leaves

PORK

GINGER & CORIANDER MARINADE

bunch of coriander

½ cup curly parsley leaves

12 basil leaves

thumb-sized piece of fresh ginger root

¼ cup olive oil

1 tsp ground coriander

1 tbsp salt

¼ tbsp cracked pepper

SMOKY TOMATO MARINADE

6 sundried tomatoes

½ cup olive oil

1 tbsp capers

1 tsp smoked paprika

1 red chilli

1 tbsp Worcestershire sauce

1 tbsp soy sauce

FISH & SEAFOOD

OREGANO & LEMON MARINADE

2 tbsp dried oregano

½ cup olive oil

1 tbsp white wine vinegar

zest and juice of 1 lemon

2 cloves garlic

½ onion

1 cup curly parsley leaves

CHILLI & LIME MARINADE

zest and juice of 2 limes

1 red chilli

½ cup pineapple juice

½ cup olive oil

½ bunch coriander leaves

1 cup coconut cream

cocktails

There's nothing like a pre-dinner cocktail, or an after-dinner cocktail to round off the night. As with cooking, make the most of seasonal ingredients – a big jug of strawberry daiquiri goes down a treat on a summer evening but wouldn't work for a winter dinner.

As far as my personal taste goes, I still can't go past a dry vodka martini with olives, shaken not stirred.

La Bella

Serves 1

45ml vanilla vodka
15ml limoncello
2 tsp sugar
juice of 1 lemon

Chill a large martini glass by filling it with ice cubes. Add all the ingredients to a Boston shaker with ice and shake until well combined and chilled. Remove the ice from the martini glass and rub the rim with a lemon wedge, then dip the rim in a saucer of sugar. Strain the cocktail into the glass.

Mid-autumn

Serves 1

30ml Cointreau
45ml feijoa vodka
3 lime segments, squeezed
mint, roughly chopped
apple juice
whole mint leaves to garnish

Shake all the ingredients except the whole mint leaves in a shaker with ice. Serve with plenty of ice in a tall glass. Garnish with the mint leaves.

Esprit

Serves 1

1 fresh strawberry
15ml passionfruit vodka
15ml strawberry liqueur
Champagne

Place the strawberry in a Champagne flute. Pour in the vodka and strawberry liqueur, then top with Champagne.

Frozen Daiquiri

Serves 6

300g frozen berries
270ml white rum
180ml strawberry liqueur
1 tbsp sugar
juice of 1 lime
sprigs of mint to garnish

Combine all the ingredients except the mint in a blender and purée until smooth. Check taste and adjust to suit (if too sweet, add more lime juice; if too sour, add more sugar). Pour into six martini glasses and garnish with sprigs of mint.

Dubonnet Rouge

Serves 6

1 punnet fresh raspberries
juice of 1 lemon
500ml Dubonnet
400ml crème de cassis
soda
mint leaves to garnish

Mash the raspberries to make raspberry pulp. Add the lemon juice, Dubonnet and crème de cassis. Divide between six short rocks glasses and top with ice and soda. Garnish with the mint leaves.

Sangria

Serves 6

550ml red wine, chilled
100ml green ginger wine
200ml Cointreau or other
  fruit liqueur
200ml cranberry juice
50ml lime juice
½ tsp cinnamon
chopped fruit, e.g. oranges,
  lemons, apples

Combine all the ingredients except the fruit in a large jug. Pour into six short rocks glasses over ice. Top with chopped fruit.

Amaretto Sour

Serves 1

60ml Amaretto
30ml lemon juice
1 tsp sugar
½ egg white (optional)
maraschino cherry to garnish

Combine all the ingredients except the garnish in a Boston shaker along with some ice, and shake vigorously. Strain into a rocks glass over ice and garnish with the maraschino cherry.

Sangria

Pineapple Sour

Serves 6

500ml chilled pineapple juice
¼ cup sugar
200ml lemon juice
mint leaves

Shake about half the pineapple juice with the sugar and lemon juice in a shaker along with some ice, until the sugar dissolves. Pour into a large jug over plenty of ice and add the remaining pineapple juice and the mint leaves. Serve in tall glasses.

Tom Collins

Serves 1

45ml gin
20ml lemon juice
2 tsp sugar
soda
lemon slice to garnish

Add the first three ingredients to a Boston shaker with some ice, and shake until well combined and chilled. Strain into a tall glass over lots of ice and top with the soda. Garnish with the lemon slice fitted on the edge of the glass.

Gin & Elderflower

Serves 1

30ml gin
20ml elderflower cordial
zest of 1 lemon
soda
squeeze of lemon juice
lemon slice to garnish

Combine the gin, elderflower and lemon zest in a tall glass over ice. Top up with soda and add the lemon juice. Garnish with the lemon slice.

French Martini

Serves 1

30ml vodka
30ml Chambord raspberry
  liqueur
30ml pineapple juice
juice of ½ a lime
twist of lemon peel to garnish

Chill a large martini glass by filling it with ice cubes. Add all the ingredients except the garnish to a Boston shaker with ice, and shake until well combined and chilled. Remove the ice from the martini glass, then strain the contents of the shaker into the glass and garnish with the lemon twist.

Pineapple Sour

tapas

Most people, including me, love to eat tapas. Small tasty morsels, traditionally simple (and not just little dishes of expensive ingredients), they can range from quickly grilled calamari to a slow-braised chorizo and bean stew; the list is endless. Try being adventurous with your serving platters or little dishes; bright Spanish colours work well – and of course terracotta looks fantastic.

Catalonian Tomato Bread

Serves 6

Make this with a baguette or rustic bread of your choice in summer when tomatoes are in full swing.

4 tomatoes

small bunch of basil

1 red onion, finely diced

1 clove garlic, finely diced

flaky salt and pepper

250ml extra virgin olive oil, plus extra for brushing bread and to serve

1 baguette

½ cup shaved Parmesan cheese

Cut the tomatoes into quarters and remove the cores, then cut into 5mm squares.

Finely slice most of the basil, then mix with the tomatoes, onion and garlic in a bowl. Season with salt and pepper and cover with the olive oil. Leave to marinate for 2 hours.

Thinly slice the bread at an angle. Brush each slice (both sides) with oil and lightly grill on both sides. Remove from the heat and top with the tomato mix, then return to the grill until the topping is warmed through.

TO SERVE

Finely slice the remaining basil, then sprinkle it over the tomato-topped bread with some shaved Parmesan. Drizzle with oil and serve immediately.

Green-lipped Mussel & Preserved Lemon Fritters

Serves 6

1 red onion, finely diced

1 red chilli, deseeded and finely sliced

olive oil for frying

½ cup chopped dill

½ cup chopped flat-leaf parsley

½ cup preserved lemons, finely sliced

15 green-lipped mussels, cooked and roughly chopped

250ml soda water

180g plain flour

salt and pepper

½ cup mashed potato, warm and seasoned

canola oil for deep-frying

Sauté the onion and chilli in the olive oil over a medium heat until soft. Add the herbs, lemon and mussels. Set aside.

Pour the soda into a medium-sized bowl. Whisk in the flour until thick and smooth, then season with salt and pepper. Fold in the mussel mixture followed by the mashed potato. Check the seasoning and adjust as required.

Pour the canola oil into a frying pan until it is 3cm deep, then heat to 180°C. Drop a small amount of the mixture into the oil to check if it is hot enough – the mixture should sizzle. Using two spoons to make oval-shaped fritters, deep-fry three or four at a time, for 4–5 minutes until golden brown, turning once.

Remove from pan and drain on kitchen paper. Repeat until mixture is used up.

Catalonian Tomato Bread

Banana Leaf-wrapped Paua with Pineapple Crisps

Serves 6

Paua (abalone) is so versatile; you can make soups, salads, burgers and fritters out of it. Here it's teamed with mainly Asian ingredients and served with sweet pineapple crisps, which are easy to cook as well as making a great serving vehicle for the paua. As for banana leaves, they are readily available from good Asian grocery stores.

1 pineapple

2 spring onions, finely chopped

1 clove garlic, chopped

½ red chilli, deseeded and chopped

canola oil for cooking

salt and pepper

6 whole paua (abalone), finely minced

1 egg

zest and juice of 2 limes

2 tbsp palm sugar, grated

1 tbsp coriander, chopped

1 tbsp mint, chopped

50ml cream

1 tsp sesame oil

100g plain flour

12 banana leaves

crème fraîche to garnish

Preheat the oven to 120°C.

Peel the pineapple and cut into 24 paper-thin slices. Arrange the slices on a non-stick baking tray, keeping them separate (do this in batches). Bake for 25 minutes, then turn each slice over. Return to the oven and bake until the slices are very crisp; much like potato crisps in texture. Set aside.

Lightly sauté the spring onions, garlic and chilli in canola oil until soft. Transfer to a mixing bowl, add the remaining ingredients except the banana leaves and crème fraîche, and mix until well combined (an electric mixer will give the best results). Check the seasoning and adjust as required.

From the banana leaves cut 24 thin strips, each about 3cm wide and 12cm long. Place an even tablespoonful of the paua mixture at one end of each strip and roll up. Seal with cocktail sticks or skewers.

Place on a non-stick tray and bake in a preheated 180°C oven for 15 minutes.

TO SERVE

Arrange 24 pineapple crisps on a serving platter and place a banana leaf package on top of each one. Top with a teaspoonful of crème fraîche.

Chilli-seared Tiger Prawns with Grey Goose Vodka Gazpacho

Serves 6

This is a dramatic way of serving prawns as an appetiser and although there are quite a few ingredients in the tomato shots, they're not that hard to make.

CHILLI-SEARED PRAWNS

12 raw tiger prawns, peeled and deveined, leaving head and a small piece of tail intact

salt and pepper

½ red chilli, deseeded and chopped

extra virgin olive oil

juice and zest of 1 lemon

4 slices parma ham, each cut into 3 lengthways

12 small sticks celery

GREY GOOSE GAZPACHO

1 small red onion, diced

½ cucumber, peeled and roughly diced

½ red capsicum (pepper), deseeded and roughly diced

1 x 400g can tomatoes

1 cup tomato juice, chilled

salt and pepper

dash of white wine vinegar

dash of Worcestershire sauce

180ml Grey Goose vodka

Tabasco sauce to taste

Season the prawns with salt, pepper and chilli, then lightly sauté in the olive oil until just cooked. Add the lemon juice and zest and allow to cool in the pan.

Wrap a strip of ham around a prawn and a stick of celery to enclose. Repeat with the rest of the prawns to make 12 wrapped celery sticks.

In a food processor blend the onion, cucumber, capsicum, tomatoes and tomato juice until the vegetables are finely pulverised. Transfer the mixture to a sieve and strain into a bowl or jug to give a smooth finish. Add salt and pepper to taste along with the white wine vinegar and Worcestershire sauce. Add the vodka and Tabasco to taste.

TO SERVE

Place two wrapped celery sticks in six tall glasses (or one each in 12 shot glasses). Fill with the gazpacho and refrigerate until ready to serve (this will make the glasses really frosty and add impact).

Crayfish Kebabs with Apple Aïoli

Serves 6

As crayfish is very meaty and packed with a lot of flavour, you can spoil it by adding too much, so it's best kept simple.

APPLE AÏOLI

4 egg yolks

60ml white balsamic or Italian white wine vinegar

½ tbsp Dijon mustard

60ml apple juice

1 clove garlic, finely diced

salt and pepper

extra virgin olive oil

2 Granny Smith apples, peeled and finely chopped

CRAYFISH KEBAB

3 cooked crayfish

2 Granny Smith apples

juice of 1 lemon

olive oil

salt and pepper

18 bamboo cocktail sticks

Make the aïoli first. In a food processor combine the egg yolks, vinegar, mustard and apple juice and process on high speed until pale and creamy. Add the garlic and a good pinch of salt and pepper and process to mix. With the motor running, slowly start adding the oil (it's easier to control the amount if you pour the oil from a pouring jug). As the oil mixes with the egg, it should combine and thicken. Add as much oil as necessary to achieve the desired consistency.

Stir in the chopped apple and season with salt and pepper to taste.

Remove the crayfish tails and slice the flesh into 36 x 5mm rounds.

Cut the apples into small segments using a small knife.

Thread two slices of crayfish onto each skewer followed by a piece of apple, making 18 kebabs in total.

Brush the kebabs with the lemon juice and olive oil, season with salt and pepper and place under a hot grill for 3–4 minutes. Turn over the kebabs and cook for a further 2–3 minutes until golden brown.

TO SERVE

Arrange the kebabs on a serving platter and garnish with the aïoli.

Pork Rillettes with Rémoulade Sauce

Serves 12

Traditionally made by slowly cooking meat in duck fat (now widely available in specialty food stores), rillettes is similar to pâté. I make it with pork belly because it has the right fat-to-meat ratio to get a tasty result.

1kg pork belly, skin on but bones removed

1 tbsp flaky salt

1 tsp cracked black pepper

1 tsp ground coriander

1 tsp ground cinnamon

1 carrot, peeled and cut into quarters

1 white onion, finely chopped

6 cloves garlic, peeled

4 apples, peeled and roughly chopped

1 swede, peeled and roughly chopped

12 sage leaves, chopped

2 litres duck fat, melted (or olive oil)

RÉMOULADE SAUCE

4 egg yolks

1 tbsp Dijon mustard

juice of 1 lemon

1½ cups olive oil

salt and pepper

2 tbsp wholegrain mustard

¼ cup chopped chives

Preheat the oven to 150°C.

Rub the pork all over with the salt, cracked pepper, coriander and cinnamon.

Place in a deep baking dish and add the remaining ingredients, ensuring the belly is totally immersed.

Bake for 2 hours or until the meat is falling-apart tender. Remove the belly and other solids from the fat and cover the fat with cling film (the fat can be reused; once cool, keep in a good air-tight container in the fridge).

When the meat and other ingredients are cool enough to handle, place in the bowl of a mixer. Using the hook attachment, mix together on a low speed just long enough so that everything is incorporated but still rough-textured. It may be necessary to add half a cup of duck fat to moisten the mixture.

Season to taste with salt and pepper, then transfer the mixture to a pâté mould or bowl. Pour a little warm duck fat over the top to seal and preserve the rillettes. Refrigerate for at least 6 hours before using.

To make the rémoulade sauce, blend the yolks, mustard and lemon juice in a food processor on high speed until the mixture becomes pale.

With the motor running, drizzle in the oil in a thin steady stream until well combined. Season to taste, then add the wholegrain mustard and chives. Check seasoning again and adjust if required.

TO SERVE

Spoon some rillettes onto a piece of toasted baguette or your favourite bread. Serve with a dish of cornichons, along with the rémoulade sauce.

Chorizo & Manchego Fritters

Serves 6

I've used chorizo and Manchego cheese in this recipe, but there are a lot of different flavour combinations you could try.

FLAVOURING

300g chorizo sausage, skin removed and finely diced

1 red onion, finely diced

2 garlic cloves, sliced

olive oil for frying

2 red capsicums (peppers), deseeded, roasted and finely diced

2 tbsp smoked paprika

salt and pepper

300g Manchego cheese, rind removed and finely diced

CHOUX PASTRY

60ml water

60ml milk

50g butter, cut into cubes

¼ tsp salt

½ tsp sugar

75g plain flour, sifted

2 eggs

Fry the chorizo, onion and garlic in olive oil over a medium heat until the onion is soft and the chorizo is cooked, but still juicy. Transfer to a bowl and add the capsicum and paprika. Season with salt and pepper and allow to cool.

Make the pastry next. In a medium-sized saucepan, combine the water, milk, butter, salt and sugar and bring to the boil. Stir, using a spatula, for 1 minute.

Remove from the heat and quickly add the flour, beating continuously with the spatula. When the mixture is very smooth, add the eggs one by one. Return to the heat and cook for 1 minute until the pastry leaves the side of the pan.

Add the Manchego cheese to the cooled capsicum mixture and mix it through the choux pastry. Roll the paste into walnut-sized balls.

Heat a deep-fryer to 150°C. Fry small batches of the fritters in the hot oil for about 6–7 minutes; they might look cooked sooner, but ensure they're cooked right through before removing from the fryer. Drain the fritters on kitchen paper, season and serve.

Tiger Prawn & Sesame Toasts

Serves 6

This revved-up version of the prawn toasts you can get at Chinese restaurants makes a great tapas dish or can be served as a starter with a spicy cucumber salad. Be careful when frying the toasts not to have the oil too hot or they may burn.

12 slices brioche or bread

2 tbsp hoisin sauce

¼ red chilli, deseeded and finely diced

250g raw tiger prawn meat, minced

salt

pinch of cayenne pepper

1 clove garlic, finely chopped

zest of 1 lemon

1 egg

50ml fresh cream

2 spring onions, finely chopped

1 tbsp chopped fresh ginger

juice of 1 lemon

1 tbsp sesame seeds

100ml canola oil for frying

3 limes, cut into wedges, to garnish

2 red chillies, sliced, to garnish

Brush each slice of bread on one side with the hoisin sauce, then sprinkle with the chilli.

In a mixing bowl season the prawn meat with the salt, cayenne pepper, garlic and lemon zest. Beat in the egg and then the cream until the mixture is smooth. Add the spring onions, ginger and lemon juice.

Using a palette knife or spatula, smoothly spread the prawn mixture about 1cm thick over the seasoned bread. Sprinkle with the sesame seeds.

Heat the canola oil in a non-stick pan and fry the bread, prawn side down, until golden brown, then turn over and cook the underside until crispy.

TO SERVE

Chop the crusts off and discard. Cut each piece of fried bread into three equal portions, then arrange on a tapas platter and garnish with the lime wedges and sliced chillies.

Roast Pears with Parma Ham, Beetroot Relish & Blue Cheese

Serves 6

Blue cheese, pears and ham were made for each other. All that's required in this recipe is a construction job, i.e. putting them together. I've added some beetroot relish, leftovers of which can be used with other dishes or in cold meat sandwiches, to provide a tangy element.

ROAST PEARS

3 large unripe pears

salt and pepper

1 litre clean duck fat

100g Parma ham, thinly sliced

BEETROOT RELISH

2 red onions, diced

2 cloves garlic, diced

olive oil for frying

2 large beetroot, cut into 1cm cubes

1 tsp mixed spice

pinch of chilli powder

1 cup red wine vinegar

1 cup sugar

salt and pepper

BLUE CHEESE DRESSING

250g Stilton or other blue cheese

50ml olive oil

1 small red onion, finely diced

bunch of chives, finely chopped

1 red chilli, deseeded and finely diced

zest and juice of 1 lemon

1 clove garlic, crushed

salt and pepper

Peel and halve the pears lengthways. Remove the cores, but leave the stems attached, then cut into quarters lengthways. Season with salt and pepper.

Place the duck fat in a saucepan and heat to 85–90°C (if you don't have a thermometer, this is just before it starts to simmer). Carefully place the pear quarters into the hot fat and slowly cook without boiling for 15–20 minutes until soft, but still holding their shape. Remove the pears from the fat and allow to cool.

Sauté the onions and garlic in the oil until soft, without browning. Add the beetroot, mixed spice and chilli powder. Cook until the beetroot is soft, then add the red wine vinegar and sugar.

Cook until the liquid has reduced and the beetroot is glazed and a little sticky. Add salt and pepper to taste, and allow to cool to room temperature before serving. This relish can be kept in the fridge for 2–3 weeks.

Preheat the oven to 180°C. Wrap each cooled pear quarter in a slice of ham, then place in a non-stick frying pan over medium heat and cook for 2–3 minutes on each side until nicely coloured. Transfer the wrapped pears to a roasting dish and finish in the oven for about 3 minutes.

Process the blue cheese in a food processor until smooth. With the motor running, slowly add the oil, taking care not to split the mixture. Fold in the remaining ingredients and season to taste.

TO SERVE

Arrange the wrapped pears in the centre of a serving dish with a spoonful of the relish on one side and a spoonful of the blue cheese dressing on the other.

Parma Ham & Lemon-coated Scallops

Serves 6

Lemon powder made from lemon rind is magical stuff provided it's not cooked in a hot oven, which will make it taste bitter. It has a very intense flavour so you only need a dusting.

4 lemons
18 large scallops
18 slices mozzarella cheese
18 basil leaves
salt and pepper
18 slices Parma ham
75ml extra virgin olive oil
2 tbsp chopped chives
½ cup diced tomato flesh
½ cucumber
olive oil for frying

Preheat the oven to 100°C.

Peel the lemons. Reserve the fruit and bake the rind until very crispy. When cold, grind in a clean coffee grinder until reduced to a powder, then set aside.

Cut the scallops in half across the middle. Make 18 'scallop sandwiches' by placing a slice of mozzarella and a basil leaf between the halves. Season with salt and pepper.

Fold each piece of ham in half and roll it around a 'scallop sandwich'. Dust the top and bottom of each 'sandwich' with lemon powder.

To make the dipping sauce, remove and discard the pith from two of the reserved rindless lemons. Roughly chop the lemons and place in a bowl with the extra virgin olive oil, chives and tomato flesh. Peel the cucumber and remove the seeds. Finely chop the flesh and add to the lemons and tomato. Season with salt and pepper.

Gently fry the wrapped scallops in olive oil over a medium heat, on both sides until light brown. Take care not to burn the lemon powder.

TO SERVE

Place the scallops on a serving platter with the dipping sauce in a bowl in the middle.

Sautéed Whitebait with Garlic, Parsley & Lemon Butter

Serves 6

New Zealand whitebait has a distinctive flavour which works really well with garlic and lemon. If using whitebait from the northern hemisphere, simply be a little more generous with the seasoning.

GARLIC BUTTER
100g salted butter, softened
50ml extra virgin olive oil
2 tbsp flat-leaf parsley
2 cloves garlic, peeled
salt and pepper

SAUTÉED WHITEBAIT
flour mixed with salt for dusting
300g whitebait
salt and pepper
olive oil for frying
zest and juice of 1 lemon
2 tbsp chopped flat-leaf parsley
1 tbsp small capers
croûtons to serve
lemon juice to serve

Place all the ingredients for the garlic butter in a food processor and pulse until well combined and the parsley is chopped.

Lightly flour the whitebait and sieve off any excess. Season with pepper. Add a little oil to a non-stick frying pan and heat to smoking hot. Add the whitebait and stir quickly in the pan over the heat. When they're about half-cooked, add the garlic butter, lemon zest and juice, parsley and capers. Cook for 2 more minutes, then remove from the heat (there will be enough heat in the pan to melt the butter and cook the whitebait right through). Check and adjust seasoning to taste.

TO SERVE
Place a small amount of the whitebait mixture on a crispy croûton and garnish with a squeeze of lemon and a drizzle of the garlic butter from the pan.

dinner

A good way to kick off a dinner party is to serve tapas and cocktails beforehand, and begin the meal itself with a light starter. Alternatively, make the tapas more substantial, then go straight to the main course.

The preparation for some of the dishes in this chapter will require a bit of time and effort, but the pay-off is that they are easy to serve (running around like a headless chicken is not a good look, especially when you are all dressed up!).

If you can add a bit of theatre to the occasion, so much the better. The papillote of strawberries and pineapple, for instance, will certainly make an impression when the bags are cut open at the table and the amazing smell of the cooking juices escapes.

Crispy Salt & Pepper Squid with Tamarillo & Chilli Dressing

Serves 6

I love the simplicity of this dish in which tamarillo and chilli work so well together. The dressing is also good with grilled or roast pork dishes, and will keep for a week in the fridge. Make sure the squid is really fresh – your fishmonger should be able to clean it up for you. If tamarillos are unavailable, ripe vine tomatoes would be a good alternative.

½ red chilli, deseeded and chopped

1 tbsp white sugar

½ cup rice wine vinegar

½ clove garlic, finely chopped

2 tbsp finely chopped spring onion

3 tamarillos, peeled and chopped

100ml sunflower oil

6 fresh squid tubes, cut into rings

flaky salt and cracked pepper

3 limes, halved

Mix together the chilli, sugar and rice wine vinegar until the sugar dissolves. Add the garlic, spring onion and tamarillo, and allow to infuse for at least 30 minutes.

Heat a wok over a medium to high heat and add the oil. Toss the squid in the salt and pepper to lightly coat, then add to the hot wok and cook for 1–2 minutes maximum.

Drain on kitchen paper.

TO SERVE

Serve the squid garnished with the lime halves and with the dressing in a dipping bowl on the side.

Steamed Pipis with Fennel & Spring Onion Udon Noodle Soup

Serves 6

For a long time pipis have been rather underrated in New Zealand, but these days more people are starting to cook with them. They are great in soup and work well with strong flavours such as the fennel and spring onion in this recipe. I've used udon noodles here, but any type of noodle will do. Substitute cockles, clams or mussels if pipis are unavailable.

1kg fresh pipis
100g butter
1 white onion, chopped
2 cloves garlic, chopped
½ Savoy cabbage, finely sliced
2 tbsp rice wine vinegar
600ml Pernod
200ml dry white wine
1 litre chicken stock
4 spring onions, finely sliced
4 fennel bulbs, finely sliced
3 tbsp chopped flat-leaf parsley
500g cooked udon noodles

Place the pipis in a bucket of fresh water for 30 minutes to allow them to spit out any sand.

Melt the butter in a large saucepan and lightly fry the onion, garlic and cabbage until soft. Add the vinegar, Pernod and white wine and bring to the boil. Add the pipis and cover the pan. Cook until the shells open, about 3–5 minutes.

Remove the pipis, reserving the liquid, and set aside to keep warm. Discard any unopened pipis. Bring the stock to a boil and add the cooking liquid. Reduce by one quarter, then add the spring onion and fennel and cook for 3–4 minutes.

Add the chopped parsley and noodles and cook until warmed through. Taste and adjust seasoning as required.

TO SERVE
Place the pipis, still in their shells, in serving bowls and arrange a mound of noodles in the middle. Pour in the hot soup and serve.

Scallops with Feta & Chervil Gratin

Serves 6

The sweetness of scallops goes so well with salty feta cheese and peppery watercress. Serve them in shells for maximum impact; your local fish shop should be able to source shells for you and, if you wash them thoroughly after each time, you can use them again and again.

18 scallop shells (bottom halves only)

36 fresh scallops

1 red onion, chopped

1 clove garlic, chopped

200ml dry white wine

zest and juice of 1 lemon

salt and pepper

400ml cream

2 tbsp chervil, chopped

2 tbsp chives, chopped

extra virgin olive oil

100g fresh watercress

120g feta cheese, crumbled

2 egg yolks

rock salt to serve

halved lemons to garnish

Make sure the scallop shells are thoroughly cleaned before using.

Combine the scallops, onion, garlic, wine, lemon juice and zest in a wide pan. Season with salt and pepper, and bring to the boil. Remove the scallops and set aside to keep warm. Continue boiling the wine until reduced by half.

Add three-quarters of the cream and simmer until reduced by one-third. Remove from the heat and add the chervil and chives.

Gently heat the oil in a frying pan and add the watercress. Stir until lightly wilted, then drain on kitchen paper.

Divide the watercress evenly between the scallop shells. Place two scallops in each shell and sprinkle with the feta.

Whisk the remaining cream until soft peaks form and fold into the sauce along with the egg yolks. Pour the creamy sauce over the scallops and place under a hot grill to glaze until golden brown.

TO SERVE

Sprinkle the serving plates with a little rock salt to stop the shells rolling around (a small clump of seaweed is another option). Garnish with lemon halves and serve with focaccia.

Squid & Cashew-stuffed Chicken with Crispy Noodle Salad

Serves 6

Squid and chicken might seem a strange pairing, but it's really just another 'surf and turf' combination.

6 free-range chicken legs,
  bones removed

2 tbsp hoisin sauce

3 squid tubes

1 egg

100ml cream

½ red chilli, deseeded and
  finely chopped

2 spring onions, finely sliced

2 tbsp chopped cashew nuts

salt and pepper

1 cucumber, peeled, deseeded
  and julienned

1 x 250g packet crispy noodles

1 tbsp rice wine vinegar

2 tbsp satay sauce

½ red chilli, deseeded and
  chopped

50ml olive oil

Preheat the oven to 180°C.

Place the chicken legs on a chopping board and, using a sharp knife, slit the flesh of each one in the centre to make a pocket for the stuffing. Generously brush the legs with hoisin sauce.

In a food processor blend the squid, egg and cream until smooth. Transfer to a bowl and add the red chilli, spring onions and cashew nuts. Season with salt and pepper and mix together well.

Place a large spoonful of the stuffing in each pocket and bring the sides up to cover and enclose the mixture. Roll up each leg in a sheet of tinfoil and fold over the ends to seal; each one should be a cigar shape.

Bake the chicken for 25 minutes, then remove from the oven and allow to rest for a few minutes.

In a bowl combine the cucumber, noodles, vinegar, satay sauce, chilli and olive oil. Season with salt and pepper and toss together.

TO SERVE

Remove the chicken from the tinfoil. Cut into thin slices and arrange in a circle on the outside of each plate. Place a mound of salad in the centre.

Tarte Tatin of Capsicums & Pancetta with Crispy Chicken Livers

Serves 6

The sweetness of the capsicums in this savoury version of tarte tatin balances the richness of the livers and sourness of the sherry vinegar. In this recipe I have given instructions for making six individual tarte tatins. However, if you prefer you could make a giant one in a large baking dish.

TARTE TATIN

butter for greasing

1 tbsp brown sugar

9 red capsicums (peppers), peeled, deseeded and cut into quarters

salt and pepper

4 slices pancetta, cut into thin strips

3 tbsp chopped thyme leaves

1 x 30cm-square sheet of puff pastry

1 egg, beaten

CHICKEN LIVERS

200g chicken livers

salt and pepper

olive oil

SHERRY VINEGAR DRESSING

1 red onion, cut into eighths

1 clove garlic, chopped

½ cup sherry vinegar

10 sage leaves, roughly chopped

½ cup extra virgin olive oil

salt and pepper

flat-leaf parsley to garnish

Preheat the oven to 170°C.

Grease a 20cm non-stick ovenproof frying pan with butter and sprinkle with a little of the sugar.

Place two of the capsicums in the pan, cut side up. Sprinkle with salt and pepper, some pancetta strips and thyme leaves.

Place the puff pastry on top, pressing down over the capsicums and against the edges of the pan to seal. Using a palette knife, cut into six portions.

Brush pastry with beaten egg, then bake for 15 minutes.

Devein the chicken livers, then season with salt and pepper and toss in a little olive oil.

Sear the livers on both sides in a hot frying pan until cooked through. Drain on kitchen paper.

To make the dressing, roast the onion with the garlic and sherry vinegar for 30 minutes at 180°C until soft. While still hot, fold in the sage and olive oil and season with salt and pepper.

TO SERVE

Turn out the individual tartes onto six plates (or, if making one large tart, cut into six portions). Arrange some livers on top of each and sprinkle with the sherry vinegar dressing. Garnish with the parsley.

Seafood & Saffron Soup 'en Croute'

Serves 6

Feel free to use whatever seafood is in season when making this Cornish soup. The good thing about it is that you can make it well in advance, then cover it with pastry and bake it when your guests arrive. This is very much a special-occasion starter, but well worth the effort.

1 white onion, finely chopped

½ cup julienned carrot

½ cup julienned leek

1 clove garlic, finely chopped

50g unsalted butter

pinch of saffron threads

3 cups dry white wine

60ml Pernod

750ml cream

salt and pepper

6 scallops

6 oysters

150g white fish, cut into 12 cubes

6 tiger prawns, peeled and
   deveined

3–4 sheets puff pastry

2 egg yolks, whisked

Lightly sauté the onion, carrot, leek and garlic in the butter until soft. Add the saffron, wine and Pernod. Bring to the boil and simmer for 5 minutes, then add the cream, season with salt and pepper and simmer for a further 5 minutes.

Divide the seafood between six deep ovenproof soup bowls, 15cm in diameter. Pour the creamy vegetable mixture over the seafood and transfer the bowls to the fridge to cool.

Preheat the oven to 180°C.

Cut six 15cm circles out of the puff pastry. Brush one side of the pastry discs with the eggwash, then place, eggwashed side down, over each of the soup bowls, pressing the edges of the pastry against the sides of the bowls. Brush the tops with eggwash, then using the tines of a fork or the tip of a sharp knife make a decorative pattern as desired.

Bake for 20 minutes.

TO SERVE
Remove the bowls from the oven and serve on large under-plates with the pastry lids intact – when your guests cut through the pastry, the smell will be amazing.

Venison & Aubergine Moussaka

Serves 6

In my take on the Greek classic, the moussaka is cooked with leek, prunes and venison instead of lamb. Make it in individual serving dishes or in one large dish and serve with an iceberg salad.

500g venison mince

200ml chicken stock

1 tbsp chopped thyme

75g salted butter

1 large leek, sliced

3 cloves garlic, chopped

100g all-purpose flour

salt and pepper

100ml cream

150g Cheddar cheese, grated, plus extra for topping

50g Parmesan cheese, grated, plus extra for topping

2 aubergines (eggplants), sliced and fried

4 tomatoes, sliced

4 large potatoes, peeled and sliced

50g prunes, pitted and chopped

75ml extra virgin olive oil

Poach the mince in the stock and thyme for 10 minutes. Strain the mince, reserving the stock, and set both aside.

To the same pan add the butter and gently sauté the leek and garlic for 2 minutes. Add the flour and cook for a further 2 minutes.

Slowly add the hot stock a little at a time, stirring to combine as for a cheese sauce. When all the stock has been added, simmer for 5 minutes, then season with salt and pepper.

Add the cream, bring to the boil, then add the cheese and cooked mince. Gently cook for 2 minutes, stirring until well combined.

Preheat the oven to 150°C.

Arrange a layer of aubergine in a large ovenproof dish. Add a layer of sliced tomato and season with salt and pepper. Spoon in a 5mm-thick layer of venison sauce, followed by a layer of sliced potato. Repeat layers in this order, finishing with a final layer of prunes, Cheddar and Parmesan. Drizzle with the oil.

Bake, covered with a lid or a layer of tinfoil, for 1 hour, then uncovered for a further 20 minutes until a golden crust forms.

Confit Duck with Miso Soup & Radish Dressing

Serves 6

French-style duck confit served with miso and radishes from Japan: this dish truly crosses boundaries. The richness of the duck works really well with the sweet and sour radish dressing – and now that duck legs and duck fat are widely available, there should be no problem sourcing your ingredients. Make your own miso soup if time allows or buy some from your local Japanese restaurant.

CONFIT DUCK

50g rock salt

pepper

2 star anise, crushed

2 whole cloves, crushed

6 duck legs

1 litre duck fat, melted

RADISH DRESSING

2 cups grated radish

3 tbsp rice wine vinegar

1 tbsp mirin

2 tbsp soy sauce

4 cups miso soup

300g tofu, chopped

30g wakame seaweed

salt and pepper

Rub the salt, pepper, crushed star anise and cloves over the duck legs, then leave to infuse at room temperature for a couple of hours.

Preheat the oven to 140°C.

Place the legs in a deep baking dish and pour the melted duck fat over them. Cover the dish with tinfoil and bake for about 3 hours or until the legs are very tender. Remove from the oven and drain on a cooling rack.

Mix the radish with the vinegar, mirin and soy sauce.

Reheat the duck legs in a 180°C oven until crisp. Meanwhile, combine the miso soup, tofu and seaweed in a small saucepan and heat over a medium heat. Season with salt and pepper.

TO SERVE

Divide the radish dressing between six bowls, reserving a little as a garnish. Place a duck leg on each bed of radish, then pour the soup around and drizzle the reserved radish dressing on top.

Braised Shoulder of Lamb wrapped in Parma Ham

Serves 6

This is an impressive way to serve slowly cooked lamb off the bone. Serve it with rustic vegetables such as puréed carrot and caramelised Jerusalem artichokes.

1.5kg lamb shoulder, boned

butcher's string

salt and pepper

olive oil for frying

4 carrots, roughly chopped

4 white onions, roughly chopped

1 bunch of celery, including leaves, roughly chopped

1 bulb garlic, unpeeled and halved crossways

1 litre red wine

4 litres chicken stock

6 sprigs of thyme

2 sprigs of rosemary

2 bay leaves

2 white onions, finely diced

2 tbsp finely chopped thyme

2 tbsp finely chopped rosemary

200g Parma ham, finely sliced

250g plain flour

6 eggs, lightly beaten

250g white breadcrumbs

6 knobs of butter

Tie the lamb with butcher's string to secure and season with salt and pepper. Heat some olive oil in a large heavy-based saucepan, and sear the lamb until golden brown on all sides. Remove from the pan and set aside.

Add the carrots, onions, celery and garlic bulb to the pan and cook until coloured. Add the red wine and deglaze the pan, then cook until the wine is reduced by half. Return the lamb to the pan and cover with the stock. Check seasoning and adjust as required.

Tie the thyme sprigs, rosemary sprigs and bay leaves together and submerge in the stock. Cover the pan with a lid and bring to a very gentle simmer. Simmer for about 2 hours until the meat is almost breaking up, then remove from the heat and allow the lamb to cool in the liquid until it is cool to the touch.

Remove the meat and strain the stock into another saucepan. Place over a low-to-medium heat and simmer until it becomes light and glossy and will coat the back of a spoon.

Heat some olive oil in a pan and lightly fry the diced onions and finely chopped herbs. Set aside.

Place the cooled lamb in a mixing bowl and remove the string and skin. Allow the meat to break apart naturally. Add the cooked onions and herbs, season with salt and pepper and mix by hand. Add a small amount of the stock, just enough to lightly coat the meat, and mix in. Taste and adjust seasoning as required.

On a large benchtop roll out a 60cm length of cling film. Place another 60cm length alongside it to make a square and overlap the edges by about 3cm. Place the lamb in the middle lengthways so you have a sausage shape about 60cm long and 5cm high. Roll the lamb up tightly in the cling film, removing as much of the air as possible. Twist both ends tightly to ensure the lamb filling is well sealed in. Refrigerate for about 30 minutes or you can leave it overnight.

Preheat the oven to 200°C.

Lay the ham on a benchtop with the slices overlapping to form a long sheet the same length as the lamb; its width should match the lamb's circumference. Remove the lamb from the fridge and unwrap it, discarding the cling film. Place the lamb on the layer of ham, then tightly wrap the ham around the meat. Using fresh cling film, once again tightly wrap the ham-encased lamb. Cut across the width to make six long cylinders and remove the cling film.

Dip the lamb ends into the flour, then egg and then breadcrumbs. Repeat twice to ensure the ends are thoroughly coated. Refrigerate for at least 20 minutes to give the breadcrumbs time to set on the lamb.

Place the lamb portions on a non-stick oven tray or dish lined with greaseproof paper. Place a knob of butter on each one and bake for 15–20 minutes, turning regularly until golden brown. While the lamb is cooking, reheat the sauce.

TO SERVE
Cut each portion in half on an angle and arrange on a dinner plate with seasonal rustic vegetables.

Winter Pudding with Caramel Sauce

Serves 6

This is my take on the classic summer pudding, but here I've adapted it for winter using a mixture of autumn fruits. If you prefer, make it using just one kind of fruit and serve it with caramel sauce or a good quality vanilla-bean ice cream.

FRENCH TOAST
500ml milk
100ml cream
4 eggs
60g castor sugar
1 tsp ground cinnamon
18 slices white sandwich bread
50g butter

FRUIT FILLING
1 apple
1 pear
1 vanilla pod
50g butter
60g castor sugar
6 dried mission figs,
    roughly chopped
6 dates, pitted and roughly
    chopped
2 tbsp clear honey
100ml cream
12 tbsp chopped walnuts

CARAMEL SAUCE
500g castor sugar
125g butter
750ml cream

35mm round pastry cutter
5-6cm baking ring

Mix together the milk and cream, then whisk in the eggs. Add the sugar and cinnamon and transfer the mixture to a shallow dish.

Using a 35mm cutter, cut out a disc from each slice of bread and dip in the egg mixture. Melt the butter in a frying pan and fry the bread discs on both sides until golden. Remove and drain on kitchen paper.

Preheat the oven to 160°C.

Peel and core the apple and pear and cut into small dice. Split the vanilla pod lengthways and place in a non-stick pan with the butter over a medium heat and lightly fry it (this will give it a toasty flavour). When the butter is foaming add the diced apple and pear and the sugar and cook until soft and golden. Add the figs and dates and cook for 2 minutes. Stir the honey into the pan and cook until it has melted. Add the cream and bring the mixture to the boil. Lower the heat and cook until the liquid has reduced and is nicely glazed around the fruit. Remove from the heat.

Place a disc of French toast in the bottom of a 5–6cm ring, top with the fruit and sprinkle with chopped walnuts. Repeat with two more layers of the same. Sprinkle 2 tablespoonfuls of walnuts over each one, gently press down and bake for 20 minutes until hot.

To make the sauce, gently caramelise the sugar in a heavy-bottomed pan until golden brown in colour. Add the butter and stir for 30 seconds. Slowly add the cream, mixing continuously while the sauce comes to the boil. Pass through a sieve.

TO SERVE
Remove the puddings from the oven and allow to cool for 5 minutes before arranging on individual plates and removing the rings to reveal well-defined layers of fruit and bread with a crunchy walnut top. Drizzle with caramel sauce and serve with your favourite ice cream.

Thin Tart of Apples with Honey Ice Cream

Serves 6

I first came across this tart when I was working at Le Gavroche. A French classic, it's very much a seasonal dessert usually made in autumn when apples are at their best. I use Braeburn apples, which are a little bit drier, and less sweet than most; they also don't go glassy when cooked.

APPLE TART

300g fresh puff pastry
1 egg, beaten
12 Braeburn apples
60g unsalted butter
150g castor sugar
60ml Grand Marnier liqueur

HONEY ICE CREAM

2 vanilla pods
1 litre milk
250g runny honey
12 egg yolks
100g sugar

Preheat the oven to 200°C.

Roll out the puff pastry to about 3mm thick. Cut out a 30cm round using a large plate as a template and crimp around the edge to create a 1cm lip. Prick with a fork and brush with the beaten egg. Transfer to a greased baking tray and place in the fridge to rest.

Peel and core the apples, then cut them in half lengthways. (You have to work quickly at this point to prevent the fruit from turning brown, but don't be tempted to place the apples in lemon water; they will absorb too much and this will ruin the tart.) Place the apple halves cut side down, then using a very sharp knife, slice off each end and discard. Cut the trimmed apple halves into paper-thin slices, but don't allow the slices to separate.

Remove the pastry from the fridge. Place one of the sliced apple halves butted up against the edge of the pastry lip. Using your fingers, fan out the slices, slightly separating them as you go, but they should still be touching each other. Repeat with the rest of the apple halves, creating a spiral effect into the middle of the tart.

Melt the butter, brush it over the sliced apple, then sprinkle the sugar on top of the butter.

Bake in the oven for 25 minutes until the butter and sugar have melted into the apples. Remove from the oven and drizzle with the liqueur.

Place a greased tray on top of the tart and very carefully turn it over onto the new tray so the tart is upside down. Return it to the oven and bake for a further 5 minutes, which will caramelise the apples (this is what makes the tart so special).

Remove from the oven and allow to cool before turning the tart the right way up.

To make the ice cream, split the vanilla pods lengthways and scrape out the seeds. Mix the vanilla seeds with the milk and honey in a saucepan and bring to the boil.

Whisk together the egg yolks and sugar in a mixing bowl until smooth and thick. Slowly add the hot milk mixture, stirring to combine. Pour into a saucepan and place over a low heat, stirring constantly until the mixture coats the back of a wooden spoon. Remove from the heat and pass through a sieve.

Allow to cool in the fridge, then churn in an ice cream machine for 10–30 minutes until firm. Alternatively, place bowl in freezer and stir occasionally until frozen.

Papillote of Strawberries & Pineapple

Serves 6

The method of cooking and serving food in a paper bag is known as 'en papillote'. I highly recommend this strawberry and pineapple combination, but you can use any seasonal fruit.

2 punnets strawberries, washed with stems and cores removed

1 pineapple, peeled and cut into chunks

6 cloves

6 star anise

6 cinnamon sticks

3 cups sugar syrup

1 cup white wine

vanilla-bean ice cream

Preheat the oven to 250°C.

Place a 30cm length of baking paper on top of a similarly sized piece of tinfoil, and cut out a large circle. Repeat until you have six double-layered circles and lay them on a work surface.

Divide the fruit between the circles, placing it to one side in each case. Add a clove, star anise and cinnamon stick to each portion. Fold over the layers of paper and foil to cover the fruit, making a half-moon shape, then fold over the edges twice to seal, leaving a 2.5cm gap at one end.

Mix together the sugar syrup and white wine. Pour about half a cup into each 'bag' and seal the gap.

Gently transfer the bags to an oven tray and bake for 12–15 minutes.

TO SERVE

Serve the bags piping hot straight from the oven with a side of vanilla ice cream. Snip open with care and enjoy the delicious burst of cooked-fruit fragrance.

late supper

To me supper is about coming home from a long walk, or perhaps a movie or show later on in the evening, to a dish that has been made in advance; ideally something comforting and not too heavy.

One of my best late-supper memories goes back to the time we lived in England when I was a kid and my family would drive from our home in the Cotswolds down to my grandparents' house in Cornwall. Without fail there would always be a big pot of soup with big chunks of beef and lots of vegetables on the stove waiting for us.

I remember lying in bed afterwards thinking I was going to pop after eating way too much.

Kalamata Olive Fingers

Makes about 40–50 small rolls

These are great filled with freshly sliced Parma ham and ripe tomatoes, then drizzled with extra virgin olive oil.

350ml warm milk

30g fresh yeast

120g butter, melted

10g sugar

2 eggs

1kg plain flour

25g salt

100g black Kalamata olives, pitted and finely chopped

olive oil for brushing

Combine the milk, yeast, butter, sugar, eggs, flour and salt in a mixer fitted with the dough hook and mix for 8 minutes. Transfer the mixer bowl containing the dough to a warm place to rest for 15 minutes, then fold in the olives.

Weigh out 30g portions, then shape into fingers and place on a greased oven tray. Leave to rest in a warm place for 25 minutes.

Preheat the oven to 200°C.

Place the tray with the fingers in the oven and reduce the temperature to 185°C. Bake for 25–30 minutes, remove from the oven, brush with olive oil and leave to cool.

Welsh Rarebit with Ham off the Bone

Serves 6

Similar to cheese on toast, this used to be served (probably still is in some places) as dessert in England. I made it for the first time when I was working at Claridge's Hotel in London, where we made it by the container load. It's important to use a good quality cheese.

2 tbsp unsalted butter

3 tbsp all-purpose flour

400ml hot milk

1 tsp flaky sea salt

½ tsp freshly ground black pepper

pinch of ground nutmeg

360g Cheddar cheese, grated

½ cup freshly grated Parmesan cheese

2 tbsp Worcestershire sauce

12 slices fresh sourdough bread

1 tbsp Dijon mustard

¾ cup wilted spinach, well drained

6 thick slices of ham off the bone, cut in half

Preheat the oven to 180°C.

Melt the butter in a small saucepan over a low heat and add the flour all at once, stirring with a wooden spoon for 2 minutes.

Slowly pour the hot milk into the butter-and-flour mixture and cook, whisking continuously, until the sauce thickens.

Remove from the heat and add the salt, pepper, nutmeg, ½ cup of the Cheddar, all the Parmesan and the Worcestershire sauce.

Place the bread slices on baking sheets and bake until golden brown or lightly toast in a toaster. Lightly spread each slice of toasted bread with a little mustard and cover with the wilted spinach. Top with a slice of ham and sprinkle with half the remaining Cheddar. Spread some cheese sauce over each slice, sprinkle with the remaining Cheddar, and bake for a further 5 minutes until golden brown.

Welsh Rarebit with Ham off the Bone

Blue Cheese & Mortadella Croque Monsieur

Serves 6

These little beauties are great for a late supper because they can be made beforehand and left in the fridge until needed. Then, when you're ready, fry them in butter or finish them in a toasted sandwich-maker if you prefer. While mortadella and blue cheese (Gorgonzola is especially good) are used here, your own favourite processed meat and cheese combination will also work. In any event, I recommend serving them with a crunchy Waldorf salad.

200g butter

12 slices brioche or bread of choice

12 slices mortadella

1 red onion, finely diced

1 clove garlic, finely diced

50ml extra virgin olive oil

180g blue cheese, crumbled

12 basil leaves

300g rocket leaves

Preheat the oven to 180°C.

Butter the bread and set aside six slices. Lay a slice of mortadella on each of the remaining slices, folding and tucking under any overhanging meat.

Heat a frying pan and lightly sauté the onion and garlic in the oil until soft. Arrange a little of the just-cooked onion and garlic on top of the mortadella, then sprinkle with the blue cheese, keeping it away from the sides so it won't spill out when it melts. Scatter two basil leaves and some of the rocket over the cheese and top with another slice of mortadella. Top each sandwich with a slice of buttered bread. Press down firmly on each sandwich.

Melt some butter in a large frying pan and fry the sandwiches, one or two at a time, until golden brown. Turn over and fry for a further 2–3 minutes then finish off in the oven for 10 minutes to ensure they are hot in the middle.

Pork & Pistachio Terrine with Fig Jam

Serves 6

The potential combinations for a terrine are endless, making them the best kind of casual entrée or main course. And investing in a good quality terrine mould makes life easy.

TERRINE

250g minced pork shoulder
250g minced chicken legs
250g chicken livers, puréed
2 eggs
150ml cream
salt and pepper
oil for frying
1 onion, chopped
1 clove garlic, chopped
50g shelled pistachios,
  chopped
¼ tsp Moroccan spice mix
¼ tsp mixed spice
¼ tsp cayenne pepper
30ml brandy
150g prunes, pitted and
  chopped

FIG JAM

2 large red onions,
  finely chopped
olive oil for frying
1 cup sugar
1 cup red wine vinegar
1 cup red wine
250g figs, chopped

Preheat the oven to 150°C.

Combine the meat and mix well. Add the eggs and whip in the cream. Season with salt and pepper.

Heat a little oil in a frying pan and sauté the onion and garlic until caramelised. Add the pistachios and spices and cook for 5 minutes. Deglaze the pan with the brandy and set aside to cool. When cool, mix with the mince and prunes to combine.

Line the inside of a terrine mould with cling film. Spoon the mixture into the mould and cover with a layer of greaseproof paper, then a layer of tinfoil.

Place the terrine in a hot water bath so that the water comes to just over halfway up the mould.

Bake for 1½–2 hours, then check the centre with a meat thermometer; it should read 78°C when ready. Alternatively, insert a fork into the centre of the terrine and hold it there briefly. Bring the fork to your lips – it should be moderately hot when cooked.

Remove the terrine from the oven. Place a weight, such as a similar-sized can or cans, on the top of the terrine (this will compress it into the desired shape) and chill overnight in the fridge.

To make the jam, fry the onions in olive oil until golden brown. Add the sugar, vinegar, wine and figs and cook until the figs are soft and the liquid reduces by half.

Transfer the mixture to a blender and purée. Cool before use.

French Onion Soup with Gruyère Cheese Soufflé Topping

Serves 6

Instead of serving this soup with the traditional Gruyère cheese croûtes, I've added a light cheese soufflé topping. The soup can be made beforehand so that only the soufflé needs attention at the last minute, making it an ideal late-supper dish.

SOUP

olive oil for frying

4 large white onions, thinly sliced

salt and pepper

1 cup white wine

1.2 litres chicken stock

1.2 litres beef stock

6 sprigs thyme

30g Dijon mustard

GRUYÈRE CHEESE SOUFFLÉ TOPPING

25g butter

25g flour

200ml cream

¼ cup Parmesan cheese, grated

¼ cup Gruyère cheese, grated

salt

6 egg whites

extra grated Parmesan and
  Gruyère cheese to garnish

In a large heavy-bottomed saucepan heat the oil over a high heat. Add the onions and cook, stirring so they don't catch and burn, until they start to soften. Reduce the heat to medium. Season well with salt and pepper and keep stirring until they start to caramelise and brown. Add the wine and swirl it around, scraping the bottom of the pan to loosen any flavoursome bits. Add both stocks and the firmly tied thyme. Bring to the boil over a high heat, then turn down until gently simmering. Cook for about 40–60 minutes until the liquid has reduced by about half and the soup has thickened. Taste and adjust the seasoning if necessary.

In a small bowl mix the mustard with a small amount of soup, then stir this mixture back into the soup. Remove the thyme and once again check and correct the seasoning if necessary. Keep the soup warm until ready to add the soufflé topping.

Melt the butter over a low heat and mix in the flour. Slowly pour in the cream, stirring until smooth and creamy. Mix in the cheese until melted, then add salt as required.

Whisk the egg whites with a pinch of salt until light and smooth and very thick.

Mix the cheese sauce with an equal quantity of egg whites until smooth. Slowly and gently fold in the rest of the egg whites, keeping the mix as light as possible.

Butter six 10cm metal food mould rings and softly spoon in the soufflé mix until three-quarters full. Bake for 5 minutes in a 200°C oven. Carefully remove the rings from the soufflés and sprinkle with the extra cheese.

TO SERVE

Pour the warm soup into six ovenproof bowls and top with the cheese soufflés. Bake in a preheated oven at 200°C for 5 minutes. The soup should be hot, the cheese melted and the soufflés light.

Manchego & Leek Parcels

Serves 6

This polenta-based pastry is very easy to use because it doesn't stretch and contract like regular pastry, plus it has a lot of flavour.

PASTRY

1 tsp salt

250ml water

200g fine-grain instant polenta

100g plain flour

¼ cup chopped flat-leaf parsley

2 egg yolks

FILLING

75ml extra virgin olive oil, plus extra for drizzling over pastry

1 red onion, finely diced

1 clove garlic, finely diced

2 medium leeks, finely sliced

6 rashers bacon, chopped

12 sage leaves, roughly chopped

200g Manchego cheese, grated

50g Parmesan cheese, grated

180g spinach, cooked and roughly chopped

salt and pepper

6 basil leaves

6 slices fresh Roma tomato

extra grated Parmesan cheese to garnish

In a saucepan add the salt to the water and bring to the boil. Add the polenta, flour and parsley and mix to a firm dough using a wooden spoon.

Set aside until cool enough to handle. Mix the egg yolks into the dough until well combined, then wrap in cling film and leave to rest for 20–25 minutes.

Roll out the pastry to 3mm thick and cut into six 15cm squares.

Heat the oil in a frying pan and lightly cook the onion, garlic and leeks. Add the bacon and cook until caramelised. Add the sage to the pan and mix well. Remove from the heat and allow to cool. Fold in the Manchego cheese, Parmesan and spinach. Season with salt and pepper.

Place a generous spoonful of the filling in the centre of each pastry square. Brush the edges with water and fold in two opposite sides so they meet in the middle, forming a rectangle. Brush the top with water and fold in the other two sides to meet in the middle, this time to form a square. Turn the parcels over so the seams are underneath and gently press them down on a greased baking tray. Refrigerate for about 30 minutes to set.

Preheat the oven to 180°C. Brush each pastry parcel with a little extra virgin olive oil. Arrange a basil leaf topped with a slice of tomato on each parcel. Drizzle with some more oil and bake for 15 minutes until golden.

Remove from the oven and sprinkle with the extra Parmesan cheese.

Pork & Prune Meatballs on Soft Polenta

Serves 6

This is a great dish to make before you go out – just leave baking the meatballs in the sauce until you're ready to eat.

MEATBALLS

1 red onion, chopped

1 clove garlic, chopped

olive oil for frying

250g pork mince

250g chicken mince

50g toasted walnuts, chopped

pinch of smoked paprika

1 egg

salt and pepper

50ml cream

100g chopped prunes

white breadcrumbs

flour for dusting

olive oil for frying

100g red capsicums (peppers),
  cored, deseeded and sliced

250ml tomato and basil
  pasta sauce

SOFT POLENTA

2 cups chicken stock

1 cup full-cream milk

1 cup instant polenta

½ cup grated Parmesan cheese

2 tbsp butter

3 tbsp chopped sage leaves

salt and pepper

shaved Parmesan cheese and
  sliced basil leaves to garnish

Cook the onion and garlic in olive oil over a low heat until soft.

Transfer to a mixing bowl and add both kinds of mince, walnuts, paprika, egg, salt, pepper, cream and prunes. Mix to combine, then add enough breadcrumbs until the correct consistency for rolling is achieved.

Roll the mixture into golf ball-sized balls and dust in flour. Add some olive oil to a hot pan and fry the meatballs, a few at a time, until golden brown.

Remove the meatballs from the pan and set aside briefly. Add the capsicums to the pan and cook until soft, then add the tomato and basil sauce. Place the meatballs and the sauce in an ovenproof dish and bake in a preheated 200°C oven for 25 minutes.

To make the polenta, combine the chicken stock and milk in a saucepan and bring to the boil. Add the polenta all in one go, using a wooden spoon to mix well and beat out any lumps. Cook for about 10 minutes over a medium heat until smooth, stirring constantly.

Add the Parmesan cheese, butter and sage, then season well with salt and pepper. Serve immediately.

TO SERVE

Place a spoonful of polenta in the centre of each serving bowl. Top with a few meatballs and cover with sauce. Sprinkle with shaved Parmesan and strips of basil.

Honey-glazed Ham & Gruyère Pithivier

Serves 8

Another classic combination, perfect for supper because you can do all the hard work earlier and just bake it fresh when you're ready. I've added spinach and capsicums to lighten it up, but if you feel like making the traditional recipe, just leave them out.

400g puff pastry

olive oil

100g spinach

2 red capsicums (peppers), roasted and peeled

300g sliced ham off the bone

300g Gruyère cheese, sliced

salt and pepper

2 egg yolks, whisked

Roll out the puff pastry to around 2–3mm thick. Using a dinner plate as a template, cut out two large circles.

Heat the olive oil in a pan and briefly wilt the spinach in it. Allow to cool. Halve and deseed the roasted capsicums.

Place one pastry circle on a greased baking tray. Arrange some ham on top about 35mm from the edge. Cover with some gruyère, some spinach, a little more gruyère and lastly some capsicum. Season with salt and pepper. Repeat these layers until all the ingredients have been used up.

Brush the exposed pastry with some eggwash. Place the second pastry circle on top, pressing down around the edges to seal. Brush the top with the remaining eggwash. Using a knife or fork, decorate the pastry on the top and around the edges. Refrigerate for at least 1 hour or overnight if possible.

Bake in a preheated 180°C oven for 35 minutes, then for 10 minutes at 130°C.

TO SERVE

Remove from the oven and allow to cool slightly, then cut into wedges. Serve with a rocket and vine tomato salad.

Baked Rice Pudding with Cinnamon, Prune & Tea Compote

Serves 6

Dessert comfort food at its best, this rice pudding is better baked than cooked like a risotto, which can make the rice very starchy. If you want to add a bit of crunch, serve it with a piece of shortbread alongside.

COMPOTE
1–2 cups Earl Grey tea, hot
24 prunes, pitted
90ml cherry brandy
100g brown sugar
1 cinnamon stick
2 star anise
zest and juice of 1 orange

RICE PUDDING
80g unsalted butter
120g castor sugar
2 vanilla pods, split lengthways
150g short-grain rice
600ml milk
600ml cream
zest of 1 lemon

Pour the hot tea over the prunes and leave to soak overnight. Next day, strain the prunes, reserving the soaking liquid.

Combine the brandy, sugar, cinnamon, star anise, orange juice and zest, and 100ml of the reserved liquid in a saucepan and simmer over a low heat until the mixture turns into a light syrup. Fold in the prunes, remove from the heat and transfer to the fridge to cool. Remove from the fridge and bring to room temperature before serving.

Preheat the oven to 150°C.

Gently melt the butter in a saucepan. Add the sugar and cook for 3 minutes. Stir in the vanilla pods and cook for a further 2 minutes. Add the rice, milk, cream and lemon zest and bring to a simmer.

Transfer the mixture to a baking dish, cover and bake for 50 minutes, stirring every 10 minutes until cooked.

Remove from the oven and allow to cool. Remove vanilla pods and discard.

TO SERVE
Place a generous spoonful of the rice in the middle of each plate and garnish with four prunes per dish. Drizzle with the prune syrup and serve with warm shortbread biscuits.

weights & measures

The following amounts have been rounded up or down for convenience. All have been kitchen tested.

ABBREVIATIONS

g	gram
kg	kilogram
mm	millimetre
cm	centimetre
ml	millilitre
°C	degrees Celsius
tsp	teaspoon
tbsp	tablespoon

WEIGHT CONVERSIONS

METRIC	IMPERIAL/US
25g	1 oz
50g	2 oz
75g	3 oz
100g	3½ oz
125g	4½ oz
150g	5 oz
175g	6 oz
200g	7 oz
225g	8 oz
250g	9 oz
275g	9½ oz
300g	10½ oz
325g	11½ oz
350g	12½ oz
375g	13 oz
400g	14 oz
450g	16 oz (1 lb)
500g	17½ oz
750g	26½ oz
1kg	35 oz (2¼ lb)

LENGTH CONVERSIONS

METRIC	IMPERIAL/US
0.5cm (5mm)	¼ inch
1cm	½ inch
2.5cm	1 inch
5cm	2 inches
10cm	4 inches
20cm	8 inches
30cm	12 inches (1 foot)

LIQUID CONVERSIONS

METRIC	IMPERIAL	US
5ml (1 tsp)	¼ fl oz	1 tsp
15ml (1 tbsp)	½ fl oz	1 tbsp
30ml (⅛ cup)	1 fl oz	⅛ cup
60ml (¼ cup)	2 fl oz	¼ cup
125ml (½ cup)	4 fl oz	½ cup
150ml	5 fl oz (¼ pint)	⅔ cup
175ml	6 fl oz	¾ cup
250ml (1 cup)	8 fl oz	1 cup (½ pint)
300ml	10 fl oz (½ pint)	1¼ cups
375ml	12 fl oz	1½ cups
500ml (2 cups)	16 fl oz	2 cups (1 pint)
600ml	20 fl oz (1 pint)	2½ cups

NOTE: The Australian metric tablespoon measures 20ml

TEMPERATURE CONVERSIONS

CELSIUS	FAHRENHEIT	GAS
100°C	225°F	¼
125°C	250°F	½
150°C	300°F	2
160°C	325°F	3
170°C	325°F	3
180°C	350°F	4
190°C	375°F	5
200°C	400°F	6
210°C	425°F	7
220°C	425°F	7
230°C	450°F	8
250°C	500°F	9

CAKE TIN SIZES

METRIC	IMPERIAL/US
15cm	6 inches
18cm	7 inches
20cm	8 inches
23cm	9 inches
25cm	10 inches
28cm	11 inches

glossary

AGRIA POTATOES
Floury, versatile golden potatoes with lots of flavour. Ideal for mashing.

BEAUMES DE VENISE
A sweet fortified wine from France's Rhône Valley.

BOCCONCINI
Small white balls of mozzarella cheese, often sold floating in bowls of whey.

BOSTON SHAKER
Two-piece cocktail shaker commonly used by bartenders.

CARAMELISE
Convert sugar into caramel by gently heating.

CELERIAC
A crunchy root vegetable from the celery family.

CHICKPEA FLOUR
Also known as 'besan'. Used mainly in batter for fritters.

CHORIZO
A spicy cured pork sausage traditionally made with smoked paprika.

CLAFOUTI
Custard-like dessert traditionally made with cherries and baked in a tart tin.

COMPOTE
Fruit poached in sugar syrup and flavoured with wine and sometimes spices.

CONFIT
A method of slowly cooking in fat.

CORNICHON
A young pickled cucumber, also known as a gherkin.

CRÈME FRAÎCHE
Matured, thickened cream with a rich velvety texture and a slightly tangy flavour.

CRÉPINE
The lining of a pig's stomach, this is used to encase meats and fish like a sausage skin.

DUCK FAT
Nutritionally similar to olive oil. Low in saturated fat. Great for roasting potatoes.

EN CROUTE
Encased in pastry.

EN PAPILLOTE
To cook something, traditionally fish, in a paper bag so that the food steams as it bakes inside the paper.

ESCALOPE
The French term for a very thin slice of meat or fish.

FONTINA CHEESE
Tangy strong-flavoured Italian cow's milk cheese.

FRESH YEAST
Small block of active ingredient used in breads and some cakes. Has a short shelf life. Available from some specialist stores and bakeries.

FRITTO MISTO
Literally Italian for 'fried mixed', it refers to a selection of small pieces of fish, vegetables or meat that have been battered and then deep-fried.

GAZPACHO
Chilled, uncooked soup made of chopped tomatoes, cucumber, onions, garlic, oil and vinegar and served cold.

GORGONZOLA
A name-controlled blue cow's milk cheese from the Lombardy region of Italy.

GRATIN
Dish browned quickly under the grill, often topped with breadcrumbs and grated cheese.

HOISIN SAUCE
Thick sweet and sour sauce made from soya beans. Used in marinades and Chinese cooking.

JERSEY BENNE POTATOES
New potatoes grown in Oamaru, New Zealand. Waxy consistency, ideal for boiling.

JULIENNE
To cut into matchstick-thin strips.

LIMONCELLO
Italian lemon liqueur often used in desserts.

MANCHEGO CHEESE
A subtle sheep's milk cheese made in the La Mancha region of Spain.

MASCARPONE
A rich double-cream cheese from Italy's Lombardy region that can be mixed with savoury or sweet combinations and which is similar in texture to clotted cream.

MEAT THERMOMETER
A thermometer used to check the internal temperature of meat to gauge whether or not it's cooked.

MIRIN
A Japanese rice wine used in cooking.

MISO PASTE
Japanese fermented soya-bean paste, used in soups, sauces and dressings.

MISSION FIGS
A smaller variety of fig grown in northern California which was introduced by Franciscan missionaries.

MORTADELLA
Lightly smoked pork sausage from Bologna.

PALETTE KNIFE
A very flexible blunt knife often used when making pastry as it easily slides under pastries or cakes.

PANCETTA
Pork belly cured for a few weeks and then air-dried for 6-8 months.

PARMA HAM
From the Italian region of Parma, this famous ham is seasoned, salt-cured and air-dried.

PAUA
Shellfish also known as 'abalone'. The edible part is the black muscle.

PERNOD
Aniseed-flavoured spirit, commonly served as an apéritif (pre-dinner drink).

PIPIS
Small bivalve shellfish, similar to clams.

PITHIVIER
Large puff-pastry tart.

POLENTA
Italian cornmeal usually accompanying meat or fish and which can be served creamy or left to solidify, then sliced and sautéed, grilled or fried.

POMEGRANATE SYRUP
Concentrated, sweetened juice of the pomegranate fruit.

PORCINI
A pungent and aromatic Italian mushroom found most commonly in North America and Europe, used to add flavour to dishes. Dried porcini, which can be soaked in a little warm water to rehydrate, are readily available and have a more intense flavour.

PROSCIUTTO
Italian-style cured ham.

RÉMOULADE
A traditional French sauce made from mayonnaise and wholegrain mustard.

RILLETTES
A method of cooking meat or fish resulting in a coarse-textured pâté.

SAFFRON
The dried red stigma from the crocus flower. Because of the intensive work involved harvesting the stigma, saffron is very expensive.

SPATCHCOCK
A chicken that is prepared for cooking by cutting it open down the backbone and flattening it.

SWEAT
Frying vegetables in a little fat over low heat to soften without colouring.

TAPENADE
A thick Provençal sauce made from olives, olive oil, lemon juice and anchovies.

TARTE TATIN
A French upside-down tart traditionally made with apples.

TERRINE
A paté or similar dish consisting of meat, game, fish or vegetables generally baked in a pottery or earthenware dish and served cold.

TRUFFLE
A highly prized fungus, generally served raw as the key element in pasta and salads or in meat preparations. Truffle oil is a low-cost way to add the flavour of truffles to dishes.

UDON NOODLES
Thick round white Japanese noodles used mostly in soups.

WATER BATH
Bowl of ingredients placed in a baking dish of hot water which allows it to cook slowly.

WHITE BALSAMIC VINEGAR
Made from grape must (pressed juice, seeds and skin) and white wine vinegar, rather than the red wine vinegar of the traditional dark variety. More subtle and less sweet than regular dark balsamic.

WHITE ONION
A popular onion for cooking. Less sweet than the more common brown onion, they are best raw or in pickles.

index

acknowledgements

Cookbooks are always put together by a dedicated team of people and *Dine In* is no exception. Once again, I have been fortunate to have a great team behind me, which has made the whole experience enjoyable.

I would like firstly to thank Louise Armstrong at New Holland for giving me the opportunity to write this book and the gentle-but-firm encouragement when things got tricky, especially towards the end. I would also like to thank Keely O'Shannessy for the inspired book design and for pushing for the final shots – it was well worth it.

Thanks to Nicola Edmonds and Jacqui Blanchard for the fantastic photography.

Thanks to that incredible chain of homeware stores Nest – specifically the Wellington and Ponsonby stores – for kindly lending props for all the photo shoots.

Thanks to Ali Spencer for getting the project off the ground.

Thanks to the team at Zibibbo, especially Anthony Shone who organised the Wellington photo shoots as well as looking after Zibibbo at the same time. To Chef Jocky Mike Shaw, you know you love Classic Hits FM.

Finally, thanks to my wife Nicola who painstakingly typed up the scrawl I called recipes into something able to be passed on to the publisher.

First published in 2009 by New Holland Publishers (NZ) Ltd
Auckland • Sydney • London • Cape Town

www.newhollandpublishers.co.nz

218 Lake Road, Northcote, Auckland 0627, New Zealand
Unit 1, 66 Gibbes Street, Chatswood, NSW 2067, Australia
86–88 Edgware Road, London W2 2EA, United Kingdom
80 McKenzie Street, Cape Town 8001, South Africa

ISBN: 978 1 86966 247 9

Commissioned and project managed by Louise Armstrong
Designed by Keely O'Shannessy
Edited by Renee Lang

A catalogue record for this book is available from the National Library of New Zealand.

10 9 8 7 6 5 4 3 2 1

Colour reproduction by Pica Digital Pte LTD, Singapore
Printed by SNP Leefung in China, on paper sourced from sustainable forests.